Congressional
Research
Service

Pakistan-U.S. Relations

K. Alan Kronstadt

Specialist in South Asian Affairs

May 24, 2012

Congressional Research Service

7-5700

www.crs.gov

R41832

Summary

In a security alliance since 2004 and "strategic partners" since 2006, the United States and Pakistan for decades experienced major shifts in the nature and tone of their relations. In the post-9/11 period, assisting in the creation of a more stable, democratic, and prosperous Pakistan actively combating religious militancy has been among the most important U.S. foreign policy efforts. Vital U.S. interests are seen to be at stake in its engagement with Pakistan related to regional and global terrorism; efforts to stabilize neighboring Afghanistan; nuclear weapons proliferation; links between Pakistan and indigenous American terrorism; Pakistan-India tensions and conflict; democratization and human rights protection; and economic development. As a haven for numerous Islamist extremist and terrorist groups, and as the world's most rapid proliferator of nuclear weapons, Pakistan presents a combination that places it at the top of many governments' international security agendas.

The May 2011 revelation that Al Qaeda founder Osama bin Laden had enjoyed apparently years-long and relatively comfortable refuge inside Pakistan led to intensive U.S. government scrutiny of the bilateral relationship, and sparked much congressional questioning of the wisdom of providing significant U.S. foreign assistance to a government and nation that may not have the intention and/or capacity to be an effective U.S. partner. Although Obama Administration officials and most senior congressional leaders spent most of 2011 consistently recognizing Pakistan as a crucial ally in U.S.-led counterterrorism and counterinsurgency efforts, long-held doubts about Islamabad's commitment to core U.S. interests deepened over the course of the year. The Pakistani military and intelligence services are seen to be too willing to distinguish among Islamist extremist groups, maintaining links to Afghan insurgent and anti-India militant organizations operating from Pakistani territory as a means of forwarding Pakistani's perceived security interests.

U.S.-Pakistan relations are fluid at present, but running a clearly negative course: still based on several national interests shared by both countries, yet marked by levels of mutual distrust and resentment that are likely to catalyze a new set of assumptions for future ties. The tenor of interactions has been increasingly negative in a slide predating a series of crises in 2011. These included a CIA operative shooting dead two Pakistanis in Lahore, bin Laden's killing, suspension of most bilateral security cooperation, a spike in Haqqani Network attacks in Afghanistan, and an incident in which two dozen Pakistani soldiers were inadvertently killed by NATO aircraft. The latter calamity led Pakistan to shut down NATO's road access to Afghanistan and demand an apology that has not been forthcoming in intervening months. Access remains closed to date.

Pakistan is among the leading recipients of U.S. aid in the post-9/11 period, having been appropriated about $24 billion in assistance and military reimbursements since 2001. FY2013 legislation in the 112th Congress would cut U.S. assistance funding significantly from both the levels requested by the Administration and from those Congress approved for FY2012. Provisions also would introduce more rigorous restrictions and certification requirements on such aid. With anti-American sentiments and xenophobic conspiracy theories rife among ordinary Pakistanis, persistent economic travails and a precarious political setting combine to present serious challenges to U.S. decision makers. This report will be updated periodically. See also CRS Report R41856, *Pakistan: U.S. Foreign Assistance*, and CRS Report R42116, *Pakistan: U.S. Foreign Aid Conditions, Restrictions, and Reporting Requirements*, both by Susan B. Epstein and K. Alan Kronstadt; and CRS Report RL34248, *Pakistan's Nuclear Weapons: Proliferation and Security Issues*, by Paul K. Kerr and Mary Beth Nikitin.

Contents

Figures

Tables

Appendixes

Contacts

Overview

A stable, democratic, prosperous Pakistan actively combating religious militancy is considered vital to U.S. interests. Pakistan is at the locus of several top-tier policy areas of urgent concern, including regional and global terrorism; efforts to stabilize neighboring Afghanistan; nuclear weapons proliferation; the Kashmir problem and Pakistan-India tensions; democratization and human rights protection; and economic development. Today Pakistan is identified as a haven for numerous Islamist extremist and terrorist groups, and is the world's most rapid proliferator of nuclear weapons, a combination that places it at the top of the international security agenda.

Pakistan has been praised by U.S. leaders for its post-2001 cooperation with U.S.-led counterterrorism and counterinsurgency efforts, although long-held doubts about Islamabad's commitment to some core U.S. interests deepened dramatically in 2011 and may be altering the nature of the relationship in 2012. A mixed record on battling Islamist extremism includes ongoing apparent tolerance of Afghan insurgents and anti-India militants operating from its territory. Pakistan's troubled economic conditions and precarious political setting combine with perilous security circumstances and a history of difficult relations with neighbors to present serious challenges to U.S. decision makers.

The Pakistani people have paid a heavy price as Islamist radicalism has spread in the country and as its border region near Afghanistan has become a haven for local insurgents, as well as Arab and Uzbek jihadists. Islamabad claims that the "war on extremism" has cost the country more than 37,000 civilian lives, nearly 6,300 security forces, and $78 billion in financial losses.[1] The U.S. National Counterterrorism Center reports there was an average of more than 26 terrorist attacks *each week* in Pakistan in 2011; only Afghanistan and Iraq suffered a higher number of incidents.[2] Pakistani officials regularly seek to remind the American audience of the country's sacrifices.[3]

May 2011 revelations that Al Qaeda founder Osama bin Laden (OBL) had found apparently years-long refuge inside Pakistan marked a new era of intensive U.S. government scrutiny of a now tense and even adversarial relationship. In September that year, the then-top U.S. military officer, Admiral Mike Mullen, issued unprecedentedly strong and public accusations that Pakistan was providing support to Afghan insurgents who attack U.S. interests. Given Mullen's strenuous efforts to develop a close working relationship with his Pakistan counterpart, General Ashfaq Pervez Kayani, the pronouncement was taken as a supreme expression of U.S. frustration.

To bookend 2011's bilateral turbulence of historic scale, in late November NATO troops in Afghanistan came under fire from two Pakistani army outposts just across the shared border at Salala. Retaliatory airstrikes left 24 Pakistani soldiers dead. A Pentagon investigation determined poor coordination and miscommunication were to blame, and that NATO troops had responded appropriately. Pakistan's government and people alike have expressed fury at what some suspect was an intentional strike. Following the incident, Pakistani officials moved to scrap and renegotiate all existing bilateral agreements with the United States related to supply lines into

---

[1] Sherry Rehman, "Pakistan and the U.S.: A New Beginning?" (op-ed), *Chicago Tribune*, May 20, 2012.

[2] See the National Counterterrorism Center database at http://www.nctc.gov/wits/witsnextgen.html.

[3] Some analysts view Pakistan's "narrative of victimhood" as being at least partly disingenuous, given the distinctions its government seems to make between terrorists who attack Pakistan and all others (see, for example, Sadanand Dhume, "Pakistan: Victim of Terrorism?" (op-ed), *Wall Street Journal*, May 18, 2011).

Afghanistan and any covert American activities inside (or over) Pakistani territory, primarily those generated early in the 2000s by the governments of President George W. Bush and President-General Pervez Musharraf. Islamabad has continuously demanded a full apology from Washington as requisite for restored cooperation.

Yet of the several ways Islamabad's anger was expressed, the most contentious has been its closure of the Pakistani ground lines of communication (GLOCs) that allow NATO supplies to transit into Afghanistan. Despite much anticipation of an imminent deal to reopen them, the GLOCs remain closed to date and the issue was blamed for overshadowing a May 2012 NATO summit in Chicago. Media reports have the Pakistani negotiators seeking as much as $5,000 per truck, or what would be a 20-30-fold increase over last year—and senior U.S. officials refusing to entertain such a fee hike while railing at perceived "extortion" and "price gouging."[4]

Only days after the failure to strike a deal on the GLOCs in Chicago, a Pakistani doctor who reportedly had participated in a CIA operation to identify bin Laden family DNA received a 33-year prison sentence for treason, perplexing an American audience and angering many, including senior Members of Congress. The Senate Appropriations Committee responded within hours by attaching a unanimously approved provision to dock $1 million from U.S. aid funding in the FY2013 State and Foreign Operations appropriation for each year of the sentence unless the doctor is freed. The Administration has stated that it saw no reason for the conviction.

In many practical respects, the cooperative aspects of bilateral relations have remained frozen in 2012, even before this most mutual exasperation in May. The two governments—and, at a lower level, the diplomatic and security agencies within them—seem at loggerheads after a grueling series of crises. Anti-American sentiments and xenophobic conspiracy theories remain rife among ordinary Pakistanis; opinion surveys find that the United States has of late replaced India as the nation least favored by Pakistanis (a significant development, given the visceral, decades-old Pakistan-India rivalry). Meanwhile, Americans tend to have increasingly poor views of Pakistan.[5] The State Department warns Americans on the high risks of travel in Pakistan, and its own diplomats face travel restrictions there. American civilians have been abducted in Pakistan over the past decade. One, Daniel Pearl, was executed.[6]

Islamist extremism and militancy in Pakistan is a central U.S. foreign policy concern. Its arguably growing influence hinders progress toward key U.S. goals, including the defeat of Al Qaeda and other anti-U.S. terrorist groups, Afghan stabilization, and resolution of the historic Pakistan-India

---

[4] "Levin and McCain: Don't Pay Pakistan Exorbitant Trucking Fees," *Foreign Policy* Cable (online), May 22, 2012.

[5] A May 2011 survey found only 2% of the American sample identifying Pakistan as a U.S. "ally." Another 11% called Pakistan "friendly," while 38% called it "unfriendly" and fully 23% identified Pakistan as "an enemy of the United States." A February 2012 Gallup survey similarly found only 15% of Americans holding a favorable attitude toward Pakistan (as compared with 75% for India), down three points from the same period in 2011 (see http://today.yougov.com/news/2011/05/23/2-call-pakistan-ally-us; Gallup results at http://www.gallup.com/poll/152735/americans-give-record-high-ratings-several-allies.aspx.

[6] See the February 2012 Travel Warning at http://travel.state.gov/travel/cis_pa_tw/tw/tw_5661.html. The August 2011 kidnaping of Warren Weinstein, a 70-year-old American development expert, from his Lahore home alarmed observers, especially because Weinstein had lived in Pakistan for seven years and appeared to have been an active friend of Pakistani economic growth. Five months later, Weinstein was reported to be in the custody of Al Qaeda-allied Lashkar-e-Jhangvi militants in North Waziristan and has since appeared in a video in which he pleads for his life and conveys his captors' demands that the U.S. government free convicted terrorists imprisoned in the United States. The White House has condemned the kidnaping but rules out any negotiations with Al Qaeda ("Warren Weinstein, Maryland Man Kidnapped in Pakistan, Pleads for His Life in Video," *Washington Post*, May 7, 2012).

rivalry that threatens the entire region's stability and that has a nuclear dimension. Long-standing worries that American citizens have been recruited and employed in Islamist terrorism by Pakistan-based elements have become more acute. Several most-wanted enemies of the United States are widely believed to reside in Pakistan, among them Al Qaeda chief Ayman al-Zawahiri, Taliban chief Mullah Omar, and Haqqani Network leader Sirajuddin Haqqani. Some American intelligence officials reportedly suspect that Zawahiri may be receiving protection from elements of the Pakistani government.[7]

Over the past year, increasing numbers in Congress have more forcefully questioned the effectiveness of current U.S. policy and the wisdom of large-scale U.S. aid. Some openly call for the curtailment of all U.S. foreign assistance to Pakistan, and legislation significantly undercutting the Administration's FY2013 aid request, as well as placing new conditionality on both aid and military reimbursements, is moving through Congress in May 2012 (see **Appendix**). Congress appropriated about $2 billion in direct aid for Pakistan in FY2012, placing it among the world's leading recipients of U.S. foreign assistance (see **Table 1**). Pakistan's Ambassador to the United States has told U.S. lawmakers that "onerous" restrictions being placed on U.S. aid will be counterproductive to the goal of restoring cooperation and trust.[8]

It seems clear that the closure of Pakistani GLOCs to Afghanistan has not been the logistical catastrophe that many pundits in both the United States and Pakistan had expected. In this respect, by keeping the routes closed, Islamabad has "played its trump card" in relations with Washington and not realized the hoped-for gains. Pakistan now risks finding itself increasingly isolated diplomatically, and working positively with the United States and NATO may be the only way to change this course. By bowing to domestic political pressures, the civilian government's negotiating strategy could see the country lose billions of dollars in foreign assistance, as well as its ability to influence post-war Afghanistan.[9]

Policy Discussion

Pre-2012 Setting

In his June 2011 announcement of a U.S. military drawdown from Afghanistan in 2014, President Obama said the United States "will continue to press Pakistan to expand its participation in securing a more peaceful future for this war-torn region" and "will insist that it keep its commitments" to neutralize terrorist safe havens in its territory. In August, Secretary of Defense Leon Panetta openly acknowledged the complicating factors of Pakistan's ties to anti-Afghan and anti-India terrorist groups, but still insisted that the United States "has no choice but to maintain a relationship with Pakistan."[10] Until the potential bilateral breakdown in 2012, many, if not most, independent observers concurred that continued engagement with Pakistan is the only realistic

---

[7] "America's Next Most Wanted," *Newsweek*, May 7, 2012.

[8] "Sherry Says Strict Congressional Curbs Won't Help US-Pak Ties," *Nation* (Lahore), May 20, 2012.

[9] Najam Sethi, "Terms of Reengagement" (editorial), *Friday Times* (Lahore), May 18, 2012; "Pakistanis Fear Being Left Too Isolated," *Los Angeles Times*, May 22, 2012.

[10] White House transcript at http://www.whitehouse.gov/the-press-office/2011/06/22/remarks-president-way-forward-afghanistan; "We Must Keep Pakistan Ties: Panetta," Agence France Presse, August 16, 2011.

---

option for the United States, although some high-visibility analysts counsel taking an increasingly confrontational posture toward Islamabad.

As part of the Administration's strategy for stabilizing Afghanistan, its Pakistan policy has included a tripling of nonmilitary aid to improve the lives of the Pakistani people, as well as the conditioning of U.S. military aid to Islamabad on that government's progress in combating militancy and in further fostering democratic institutions. However, in July 2011, the Administration suspended up to $800 million in planned security assistance to Pakistan and appears to be more rigorously evaluating Pakistan's cooperation and progress before releasing further aid. At least $1 billion in approved "coalition support fund" (CSF) reimbursements to Pakistan also remains undisbursed due to bilateral disagreements and acrimony.

Developments in 2011 have seemed to validate a preexisting view of many observers that Pakistani behavior is unlikely to change given the long-held geostrategic perspectives of decision makers in Islamabad and Rawalpindi, home of the Pakistan Army's GHQ. If true, this means Pakistan will continue to tolerate safe havens for "friendly" militant groups regardless of U.S. aid levels or overt threats.[11] By many accounts, Pakistan's apparently schizophrenic foreign policy behavior is a direct outcome of the Pakistan military's perceived strategic interests. This leads analysts to encourage full-throated U.S. support for Pakistan's civilian authorities as the only viable means of reducing conflict both inside Pakistan and between Pakistan and its neighbors. The current U.S. Ambassador to Pakistan, Cameron Munter, is among those who has insisted that Pakistan requires a strong civilian government and that common U.S.-Pakistan successes can be achieved only "with a strong partner in Pakistan's democratically elected government."[12]

Still, now four years after their seating, there are few signs that Pakistan's civilian leaders are willing and able to seriously address the outcomes of their country's security policies and move them in the direction of moderation. Even in domestic discussions these leaders continue to shirk responsibility for increased rates of extremism there, and to place the bulk of blame on the United States. This perspective—apparently widespread among the Pakistani public, as well—arguably omits enthusiastic *official* Pakistani participation in supporting Islamist militancy in the region (including the provision of vital support to Afghanistan's Taliban regime throughout most of the 1990s). By nearly all accounts, this support continues, albeit selectively, to date.

President Obama has not visited Pakistan while in office, and his decision to travel to India in 2010 without any stops in Pakistan exacerbated anxiety among Pakistani officials who see signs of a "pro-India" tilt in Washington as destabilizing for the region. By refraining from engagement in the Kashmir dispute, moving forward with U.S.-India civil nuclear cooperation without any similar offer to Pakistan, and seeming to sympathize with New Delhi's perspective on the root sources of regional terrorism, the Administration's India policies are viewed suspiciously and even as threatening by Pakistani leaders and citizens, alike. Moreover, Afghanistan's October 2011 choice to establish closer and more overt ties with India, Pakistan's primary rival, and the ensuing May 2012 U.S.-Afghanistan tie-up, is grist for those figures—most especially within Pakistan's security institutions—who argue that Pakistan increasingly is under threat of strategic encirclement by external forces that seek to weaken and perhaps dismember the country.

---

[11] Timothy Hoyt, "Pakistan, an Ally by Any Other Name," *Proceedings*, July 2011; "Pakistan Unlikely to Help the US in War," Associated Press, September 23, 2011.

[12] "Sen. John Kerry Holds a Hearing on the Nomination of Cameron Munter to be Ambassador to Pakistan," CQ Transcriptions, September 23, 2010.

Debate Over Future Policy Options

The tumultuous events of 2011, peaking as they did with the Salala incident and resulting Pakistani fury, may combine to mark the end of the "post-9/11 period" of bilateral relations. For 2012 and beyond, many analysts foresee a far more narrow, issue-based engagement—often referred to as "transactional ties"—and a setting aside of the kind of broad strategic partnership envisioned by the late Amb. Richard Holbrooke, President Obama's original Special Representative for Afghanistan and Pakistan. In the January 2012 words of Pakistan's top military spokesman, "From here on in we want a very formal, business-like relationship. The lines will be drawn. There will be no more of the free run of the past, no more interpretation of rules. We want it very formal with agreed-upon limits."[13] Movement of FY2013 congressional legislation suggests such limits will include new restrictions on U.S. foreign assistance to Pakistan.

Many analysts appear to foresee a "transactional" relationship as the best realistic alternative to a potential slide into noncooperation on both sides. A more focused, issues-based engagement might better address and serve the interests of both governments, in part by bringing greater transparency and credibility to the alliance.

Ambassador Sherry Rehman, Pakistan's latest envoy to the United States, was appointed in late November 2011.[14] In an opinion piece published just before the Chicago summit opened, Amb. Rehman set forth Islamabad's prerequisites for "resetting" the bilateral relationship to include (1) apologizing for the Salala incident; (2) releasing suspended CSF reimbursements; (3) increasing counterterrorism intelligence sharing; (4) halting drone strikes; and (5) shifting to a policy of "trade not aid" by enhancing Pakistan's access to U.S. markets.[15]

Two former U.S. diplomats—agreeing that the outlook is poor for any "strategic bond" as sought over the past decade—counsel the forging of a more normal, but constructive relationship by reducing mutual expectations; reducing, but better targeting, U.S. economic aid programs; fostering more substantive business ties between the two countries; and offering more energetic, if discreet, U.S. support for initiatives that could promote regional stability, including those between Pakistan and India, and perhaps even to include dropping U.S. opposition to the Iran-Pakistan gas pipeline project.[16]

Another South Asia expert and former advisor to Amb. Holbrooke finds reason for optimism in the more humble domestic status of the Pakistani military (and the corresponding benefits this entails for democratization), and improvements in Pakistan-India relations. He urges the Obama Administration to take account of these factors and not overemphasize a purely security-oriented

---

[13] Maj. Gen. Athar Abbas quoted in "Pakistan, US Assume Less Cooperation in Future," Associated Press, January 2, 2012.

[14] Rehman was appointed in late November 2011 after the essentially forced resignation of Husain Haqqani. Rehman, a prominent former journalist and human rights advocate, was close to Benazir Bhutto and is among the government's few vocal proponents of moderation. As a parliamentarian, she authored key legislation such as the Women's Empowerment Bill, the Anti-Honor Killings Bill, the Domestic Violence Prevention Bill, and the Hudood Repeal Bill. She was also at the forefront of (thus far failed) efforts to reform the country's controversial blasphemy laws.

[15] Sherry Rehman, "Pakistan and the U.S.: A New Beginning?" (op-ed), *Chicago Tribune*, May 20, 2012.

[16] Teresita and Howard Schaffer, "Resetting the U.S.-Pakistan Relationship," *Foreign Policy* (online), March 19, 2012.

approach that could risk derailing such positive trends by eliciting even stronger anti-American nationalism among the Pakistani people and thus restoring credibility to the military.[17]

In the view of many U.S. analysts, Pakistan's May 2012 intransigence on the issues of GLOCs and insistence on an apology for Salala may prove costly and represent a missed opportunity to work cooperatively with the United States in the region. One commentator who argues this urges the U.S. government to stay firm in pressuring Islamabad on counterterrorism, especially with Pakistan's leverage reduced. Another sees Pakistan's unrelenting stance being "a catastrophic mistake" and "a triumph of short-term thinking over long-term, of scheming over strategy."[18]

Even before the post-Salala breakdown of relations, some high-profile analysts were calling for a new U.S. policy to shift to a more adversarial posture toward Pakistan on the assumption that President Obama's (and President George W. Bush's) engagement policies have failed. One senior commentator suggests "focused hostility" toward Pakistan that would hold its military and intelligence services accountable while not harming the Pakistani people more generally. This could entail targeting individuals for sanction, as well as sharply cutting military aid. Another goes further, contending that Pakistan should be considered an enemy of the United States, at least as far as Afghanistan policy is concerned, the logic being that open admission of core disagreement on this issue would benefit both countries. A third argues that only credible threats to end all assistance to Islamabad and "retaliate" if Pakistan fails to comply with U.S. demands will convince Pakistani leaders that genuine cooperation is in their best interests.[19]

Another former Holbrooke advisor is among those who reject any such U.S. shift to a more adversarial approach as counterproductive and likely to put the entire U.S.-led project in Afghanistan at risk of failure. A Washington-based Pakistani analyst likewise views a "two Pakistans" approach as unworkable and misguided, contending that U.S. policies aimed at exploiting an internal Pakistani disconnect would likely strengthen that country's conservative Islamist elements and further fuel anti-American sentiments. Instead, this observer asserts that a more "passive" U.S. approach rooted in the provision to Islamabad of security assurances and targeted efforts to bolster Pakistan's civilian governance institutions would be most prudent.[20]

It remains to be seen whether the Pakistani military's willingness to abide the current, largely economic rapprochement with India is a tactical choice to ease security and international diplomatic pressure on Pakistan, or if it represents a more strategic shift in Rawalpindi's perspective. Even if Pakistan is well positioned to enjoy the tactical "victory" that (it believes) would come through realization of a pliable, heavily Pashtun-influenced post-NATO government in Kabul, the country's geostrategic status could well suffer from the international isolation that might ensue. Many commentators offer that a rapidly changing South and Central Asian calculus should propel the Pakistani state to favor energy and trade cooperation with its neighbors over its traditional focus on conflict with India, "strategic depth" in Afghanistan, and the status of Kashmir. In this way, Pakistan might transcend the perpetual insecurity that has marked most of

---

[17] Vali Nasr, "Pakistan Spring Emerging From Winter of Discontent" (op-ed), Bloomberg News, April 15, 2012.

[18] Lisa Curtis, "Pakistan Missed Opportunity to Repair Ties With U.S.," Heritage Foundation Issue Brief #3613, May 22, 2012; David Ignatius, "Pakistan's Blown Chance" (op-ed), *Washington Post*, May 17, 2012.

[19] Bruce Riedel, "A New Pakistan Policy: Containment" (op-ed), *New York Times*, October 15, 2011; Anatol Lieven, "With A Friend Like This" (op-ed), *New York Times*, November 1, 2011; Stephen Krasner, "Talking Tough to Pakistan," *Foreign Affairs* (online), November 29, 2011.

[20] Alexander Evans, "Tough Talk is Cheap," *Foreign Affairs*, May/June 2012; Moeed Yusuf, "Fixing Pakistan's Civil-Military Imbalance: A Dangerous Temptation," U.S. Institute of Peace Peace Brief 125, May 3, 2012.

its existence.[21] The worldview of Pakistan's security services and, to some extent, domestic public are hindrances to a more robust pursuit of such policies by the country's civilian leaders.

Notable Developments in 2011

High-Profile Political Assassinations

On January 4, 2011, Salman Taseer, the governor of Punjab province, was assassinated by a member of his own security team. A senior figure in the national coalition-leading Pakistan People's Party (PPP), Taseer was among the country's most liberal politicians, and he had incurred the wrath of Islamists and other conservatives with vocal criticisms of the country's controversial blasphemy laws. His killer, Malik Mumtaz Qadri, was since lauded as a hero by significant sections of Pakistani society, and even leaders of the country's majority Barelvi Muslim sect, usually considered to hold moderate interpretations of Islam, were vocal supporters of the assassin. Taseer's assassination, strongly condemned by Secretary of State Hillary Clinton, was a major blow to liberal forces in Pakistan.

Meanwhile, on March 2, 2011, gunmen ambushed the car of Minorities Minister Shabaz Bhatti—the federal cabinet's only Christian member—and shot him to death. Bhatti had long campaigned for tolerance toward Pakistan's religious minorities and had, like Governor Taseer, openly called for reform of the blasphemy laws. Secretary Clinton expressed being "shocked and outraged" by Bhatti's killing, calling it "an attack on the values of tolerance and respect for people of all faiths and backgrounds championed by Mohammed Ali Jinnah, Pakistan's founding father."[22] Prime Minister Yousef Raza Gilani was the only senior government official to attend Bhatti's funeral. President Zardari addressed the two assassinations with an English-language op-ed in which he contended that, "A small but increasingly belligerent minority is intent on undoing the very principles of tolerance upon which [Pakistan] was founded."[23] Despite such claims, the Taseer and Bhatti assassinations and subsequent events were widely seen as evidence that Islamist radicalism is increasing in Pakistan.[24]

The Raymond Davis Affair

On January 27, 2011, Raymond Davis, an American working at the U.S. Consulate in Lahore, shot and killed two men who approached his vehicle in urban traffic. Davis contends he acted in self-defense when the men tried to rob him at gunpoint. However, Pakistani authorities accused Davis of murder and a court barred the government from releasing him despite insistence from top U.S. officials that diplomatic immunity shielded him from prosecution. President Obama

---

[21] A representative example of this argument is Sunil Datta, "Pakistan Stands Isolated in South Asia" (op-ed), *Daily Times* (Lahore), April 21, 2012.

[22] See the U.S. Embassy's March 2, 2011, release at http://islamabad.usembassy.gov/pr-11030205.html.

[23] Asif Ali Zardari, "In Pakistan, Standing Up to Extremists" (op-ed), *Washington Post*, March 6, 2011.

[24] In a sign that the Pakistani public largely supports "Islamization" more generally, a May 2011 poll found fully two-thirds of respondents answering "yes" to the question, "Should the government take steps to 'Islamize' society?" Nearly 30% thought the government should take steps toward Islamization "all at once" (see http://www.gallup.com.pk/pollsshow.php?id=2011-05-31).

described Davis as being "our diplomat."[25] Only more than three weeks after the incident did the U.S. government admit that Davis was in fact a CIA contractor and member of a covert team that was tracking militant groups inside Pakistan.

The controversy around Davis's legal status led some in Congress to openly suggest that U.S. assistance to Pakistan might be reduced or curtailed if the case was not resolved in a satisfactory manner.[26] In mid-February, Senate Foreign Relations Committee Chairman Senator Kerry traveled to Islamabad in an effort to reduce escalating tensions, taking the opportunity to express the "deepest sorrow" felt by top U.S. leaders at the loss of life.[27]

In late February, the CIA opened direct negotiations with the ISI in an effort to secure Davis's release. On March 16, 2011, after weeks of closed-door negotiations, political pressure by Pakistani officials on the courts, and, finally, a pledge of $2.3 million in *diyat*, or "blood money," for the victims' families, Davis was freed and flown out of the country.[28] Top U.S. officials denied there had been any *quid pro quo* arrangement related to Davis's release or that the United States had provided the financial compensation.

Death of Osama bin Laden[29]

On May 2, 2011, Al Qaeda founder Osama bin Laden was located and killed in the mid-sized Pakistani city of Abbottabad, a military cantonment in the northwest Khyber Paktunkhwa province, in a compound one-half mile from the country's premier military academy and just 35 miles north of the capital of Islamabad (see **Figure 1**). The location and circumstances of OBL's death exacerbated Washington's long-held doubts about Pakistan's commitment to the ostensibly shared goals of defeating religious extremism, and brought calls to curtail U.S. assistance to Pakistan. The news of OBL's whereabouts led to immediate questioning of Pakistan's role and potential complicity in his refuge. President Obama's chief counterterrorism advisor, John Brennan, told reporters it was "inconceivable that Osama bin Laden did not have a support system" in Pakistan.[30]

For a wide array of observers, the outcome of the years-long hunt for OBL left only two realistic conclusions: either Pakistani officials were at some level complicit in hiding the fugitive, or the country's military and intelligence services were grossly incompetent in their search for top Al Qaeda leaders. In either case, after many years of claims by senior Pakistani officials—both civilian and military—that most-wanted extremist figures were finding no refuge in their country, Pakistan's credibility suffered a serious blow.[31]

---

[25] "Press Conference by the President," White House transcript, February 15, 2011.

[26] H.Res. 145 called for a "freeze" on all monetary assistance to Pakistan until such time Davis was released (the resolution did not emerge from committee).

[27] See the U.S. Embassy's February 16, 2011, release at http://islamabad.usembassy.gov/pr-110216004.html.

[28] *Diyat* is a tenet of Islamic law sanctioned by Pakistani jurisprudence and reportedly used in at least half of homicide cases there ("'Blood Money' Tradition Might Help Resolve U.S.-Pakistani Row," *Los Angeles Times*, March 13, 2011).

[29] For broader discussion, see CRS Report R41809, *Osama bin Laden's Death: Implications and Considerations*, coordinated by John Rollins.

[30] Quoted in "Osama Bin Laden Killed in U.S. Raid, Buried at Sea," *Washington Post*, May 2, 2011.

[31] A listing of some of the oftentimes categorical, high-profile Pakistani denials about OBL specifically are in "Osama bin Who?," *Foreign Policy* (online), May 2, 2011.

Figure 1. Map of Pakistan

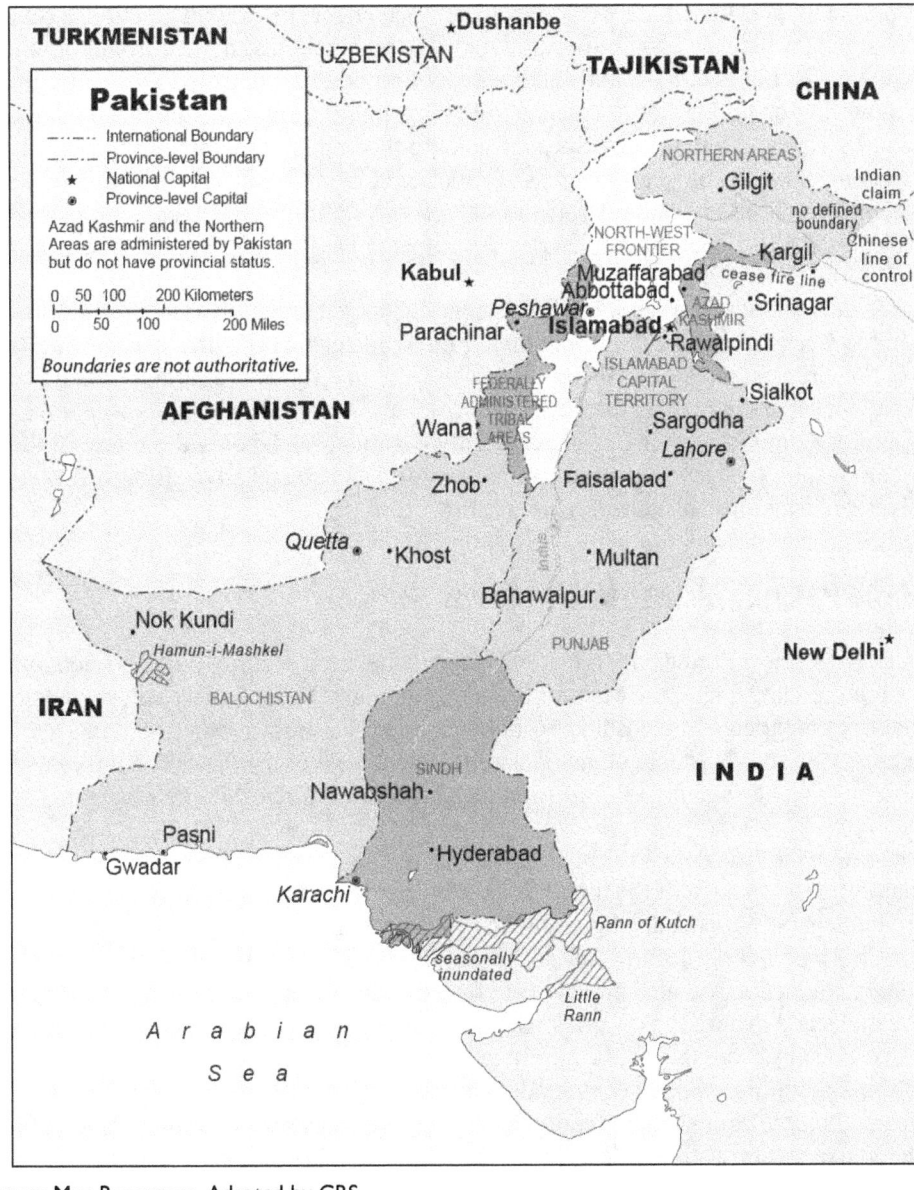

Source: Map Resources. Adapted by CRS.

Pakistan's military and intelligence services came under rare domestic criticism for being unable to detect and intercept a foreign military raid deep inside Pakistani territory, and for ostensible incompetence in detecting the presence there of the world's most-wanted terrorist. Army Chief Gen. Kayani warned that Pakistan would not tolerate any future incursions. Parliament subsequently issued a strong condemnation of the U.S. raid and again called for a halt to U.S.-launched drone strikes in western Pakistan. It also threatened to close land lines of communication through Pakistan that were considered vital to supplying NATO troops in Afghanistan. Meanwhile, public demonstrations took a bellicose, anti-American cast.[32]

---

[32] A May 2011 Gallup survey found that more than eight in ten Pakistanis who were aware of the U.S. operation (continued...)

The developments fueled bilateral distrust and acrimony unseen in the post-2001 period. Congress pointedly questioned the wisdom of continued engagement with a national government that may at some levels have had knowledge of OBL's whereabouts; figures from both major parties expressed disbelief at Pakistan's allegations of ignorance and called for greater oversight and accountability for future U.S. assistance to Pakistan. Still, senior Members tended to take a more measured view, with the House Speaker voicing the opinion that circumstances called for "more engagement [with Pakistan], not less."[33] Such sentiments tracked well with the view of many independent observers that—despite ample reasons for discouragement and distrust—the United States has had no choice but to continue to engage Pakistan in "a bad marriage."

President Obama and other top U.S. officials maintained a generally positive posture toward Pakistan in the weeks following the Abbottabad raid, while also noting that serious questions had arisen over the circumstances of OBL's refuge. The U.S. government reportedly has no conclusive evidence indicating that official Pakistan was aware of bin Laden's whereabouts. Privately, senior Administration officials reportedly became divided over the future of the bilateral relationship, with some at an apparent loss for patience and advocating strong reprisals for perceived Pakistani intransigence.

Attack on Pakistan's Mehran Naval Station

On May 22, 2011, a team of heavily armed militants penetrated security barriers and stormed Pakistan's premier naval base, the Mehran Naval Station near Karachi. Ten security personnel and four militants were killed in the ensuing 16-hour-long gun battle; two other militants are believed to have escaped before Pakistani commandos regained control of the base. The militants were able to destroy two U.S.-supplied P-3C Orion maritime patrol aircraft in their hangar.

The attack, which the Pakistani Taliban claimed was revenge for the killing of bin Laden, was the second major embarrassment of the month for the beleaguered Pakistani military, which seemed at a loss to explain how such a damaging breach could occur. The ability of a handful of attackers to wreak such havoc left the security services open to scathing criticism from the generally pro-military Pakistani media, and also brought into question the safety and security of Pakistan's nuclear weapons and materials.[34] Suspicions quickly arose that the base's attackers had inside help, given especially their ability to carefully avoid detection and take effective cover once inside. Within days a former navy commando was arrested in connection with the case. Three navy officers, the base commander among them, are to be court-martialed on charges of negligence in connection with the attack, an unusual disciplinary action for the Pakistani military demonstrating the seriousness of the breach.[35]

(...continued)

disapproved of it; only 13% approved. A majority opined that OBL should have been captured alive. The unaffiliated Gallup Pakistan found 51% of Pakistanis saying they were "sad" about OBL's death (Gallup data at http://www.gallup.com/poll/147611/pakistanis-criticize-action-killed-osama-bin-laden.aspx; Gallup Pakistan data at http://www.gallup.com.pk/Polls/16-05-11.pdf).

[33] Quoted in "Boehner: US Should Not Back Away From Pakistan," Associated Press, May 3, 2011.

[34] "Pakistan Military Faces New Questions After Raid," *New York Times*, May 24, 2011; "Pakistan Media Ridicules Military After Attack," Reuters, May 24, 2011. The growth of Pakistan's nuclear arsenal and infrastructure only increases the potential threat posed by determined militants (see Shaun Gregory, "Terrorist Tactics in Pakistan Threaten Nuclear Weapons Safety," *CTC Sentinel*, June 2011).

[35] "Three Pakistani Naval Officers to Be Court Martialed Over Base Attack," *New York Times*, August 4, 2011.

Torture and Killing of Journalist Syed Saleem Shahzad

Inter-Services Intelligence (ISI), Pakistan's main intelligence agency, is accused of ordering the torture and murder of investigative journalist Syed Saleem Shahzad, who disappeared in May 2011 just after penning an article suggesting that the Mehran attack was carried out because the Pakistan Navy was trying to crack down on Al Qaeda cells that had infiltrated the service. Shahzad, whose writing had riled the Pakistani establishment repeatedly in the past, reportedly had received numerous threats from the ISI. In a rare public statement, the ISI denied playing any role in Shahzad's fate. A closed government inquiry into the death began in June; unnamed U.S. officials later said there was sufficient classified intelligence to conclude that senior ISI officials had directed the brutal attack on Shahzad in an effort to silence critics. Soon after, then-Joint Chiefs Chairman Admiral Mike Mullen went on record with the claim that Shahzad's killing "was sanctioned by the [Pakistani] government."[36]

In January 2012, an official Commission of Inquiry reported to the Pakistani government that it was unable to identify the culprits behind Shahzad's murder while also recommending that the country's intelligence agencies "be made more law-abiding through a statutory framework carefully outlining their respective mandates and roles" and that they be made "more accountable through effective and suitably tailored mechanisms of internal administrative review, Parliamentary oversight, and judicial redressal of citizens' grievances against them."[37]

Partial Suspension of U.S. Security Assistance

In July 2011, the Obama Administration made some significant changes in its security-related aid policy toward Pakistan. According to congressional and State Department sources, $440-$500 million worth of scheduled counterinsurgency (COIN) training and equipment for Pakistan was put under suspension due to the recently reduced U.S. military trainer presence there, along with obstacles to fulfilling other agreements between the two countries. In addition, Islamabad's delays in processing U.S. visa requests led to the suspension of $300 million in planned FY2011 Coalition Support Fund reimbursements. Although the Administration presented the move as being necessitated by technical factors, observers saw it as a message and warning to Islamabad that key assistance spigots could close in the absence of improved cooperation.

A Pakistani military spokesman dismissed the development as having no effect on his organization's ability to conduct future combat operations, and he repeated the Army Chief's suggestion that more U.S. security assistance be reprogrammed toward development projects in Pakistan.[38] In the view of some observers, the Administration's decision was more likely to elicit greater resentment than greater cooperation from Pakistani leaders, and could be taken as validation by ordinary Pakistanis who see the United States as a fickle and unreliable ally.[39]

---

[36] "U.S. Admiral Ties Pakistan to Killing of Journalist," *New York Times*, July 8, 2011.

[37] "Report of the Commission of Inquiry Concerning the Gruesome Incident of the Abduction and Murder of Syed Saleem Shahzad," January 10, 2012, at http://app.com.pk/en_/images/pdf/report.pdf. A Human Rights Watch response accused the Commission of failing to interview key military intelligence officials in the course of its investigation, and of appearing "fearful of confronting the ISI" over the issue. The Pakistan military in turn reiterated a firm denial of ISI involvement and accused HRW of "choking under heaps of bias (Human Rights Watch, "Pakistan: Shahzad Commission Results Marred By Free Ride for ISI," January 30, 2012; ISPR release, February 16, 2012).

[38] "Pakistan Says It Doesn't Need US Military Aid," *Christian Science Monitor*, July 11, 2011.

[39] "In Pakistan, Many Say Aid 'Snub' Dims US Sway," Associated Press, July 11, 2011.

"Memogate" and Domestic Civil-Military Tensions

In October 2011, Pakistani-American businessman Mansoor Ijaz penned a high-visibility op-ed piece that made passing reference to a memorandum allegedly "dictated" to him in May 2011—only days after bin Laden's death—by then-Pakistani Ambassador to the United States, Husain Haqqani.[40] The unsigned memo was meant for the eyes of J.C.S. Chief Adm. Mullen, and it bluntly requested U.S. assistance in averting an allegedly imminent military coup, as well as U.S. support for Islamabad's civilian government to install friendly new leaders for the country's military and intelligence services, leaders who would fully cooperate with U.S. counterterrorism efforts. Once uncovered, the Pakistani Supreme Court, with the military's prodding, launched an investigation to reveal the actual author and purpose of the document, and the resulting "Memogate" scandal cost Haqqani his job and brought immense pressure on President Asif Zardari.[41] Both Zardari and Haqqani deny any involvement in the memo's authorship.

Ijaz was shown to be a less-than-credible witness and, while it is still incomplete, the investigation largely fizzled out when testimony did not appear to find evidence of wrongdoing by the civilians.[42] Amb. Haqqani was subsequently allowed to leave Pakistan. Yet the civil-military clash brought substantive concerns that President Zardari might face overthrow by the military. In mid-December, Pakistan's senior-most army and intelligence officers submitted to the Supreme Court statements that the memo was genuine and represented evidence of a conspiracy against the army. Prime Minister Gilani responded with an open warning that "conspiracies are being hatched to pack up the elected government" and said that the military "cannot be a state within a state" and is "answerable to parliament."[43]

Rumors of an impending military coup were so ubiquitous in December that the army publically pledged to continue supporting democracy; Gen. Kayani was quoted as saying all such rumors were "speculation." Still, during the final week of 2011, the civilian government remained infuriated that both the army and intelligence chiefs had circumvented them in engaging the court. Prime Minister Gilani again called the move unconstitutional and illegal, a claim denied by the equally infuriated military.[44]

Despite widespread alarm about the status of Pakistan's democratic government, the Pakistani public appears increasingly averse to another round of direct military rule and, unlike in the past, opposition politicians are not seeking the military's help. Add to this an assertive judiciary and a vocal watchdog media, and the odds of Pakistan seeing a military coup in the foreseeable future

---

[40] Mansoor Ijaz, "Time to Take On Pakistan's Jihadist Spies" (op-ed), *Financial Times* (London), October 10, 2011; "Pakistani Businessman Says 'Coup' Memo Was Dictated," Reuters, November 18, 2011. The document itself is at http://www.foreignpolicy.com/files/fp_uploaded_documents/111117_Ijaz%20memo%20Foreign%20Policy.PDF.

[41] Amb. Haqqani was for a period prohibited from leaving Pakistan. The alleged "ongoing harassment and mistreatment" he suffered was decried by at least three U.S. Senators, who called on Islamabad authorities to resolve the matter in ways consistent with civilian rule of law (see their January 5, 2012 statement at http://lieberman.senate.gov/index.cfm/news-events/news/2012/1/statement-of-senators-lieberman-mccain-kirk-on-husain-haqqanis-mistreatment-in-pakistan.

[42] "The Fizzling Out of Memogate" (editorial), *Express Tribune* (Karachi), February 1, 2012.

[43] "Pakistan's Memo Scandal Pits Military Against Zardari Government," *Washington Post*, December 16, 2011; Gilani quoted in "Pakistani Premier Warns of Plotting by Military," *New York Times*, December 22, 2011.

[44] See the ISPR's January 11, 2012, release at http://www.ispr.gov.pk/front/main.asp?o=t-press_release&date=2012/1/11.

---

are considered quite low.[45] By January's end, Parliament passed a resolution reaffirming its own supremacy and calling on the army and Supreme Court to remain within their constitutional limits. Gilani subsequently softened his criticisms of the military and the crisis atmosphere faded.

Salala Border Incident

In the early, moonless morning hours of November 26, 2011, U.S. ground forces on a mission very near the Afghanistan-Pakistan border reportedly came under heavy machine gun and then mortar fire from hilltop positions just inside Pakistan. According to the Pentagon, U.S. commanders on the ground had no awareness that two small Pakistan army outposts were in the area and thus believed they were being attacked by Afghan insurgents. NATO air assets were called in as a "show of force," but the incoming fire did not cease, so an AC-130 gunship, two F-15 jets, and two AH-64 Apache helicopters were ordered to neutralize the hilltop positions. By this time, Pakistani liaison officers were telling their American counterparts that Pakistani soldiers were coming under fire, but 24 of these soldiers were killed before the air assault ended. Pakistanis both official and otherwise were infuriated; some openly accused NATO forces of intentionally killing Pakistanis. Prime Minister Gilani described the attacks as being "a grave breach of Pakistan's sovereignty" and "a flagrant violation of international law."[46]

Pakistani anger, which has not subsided to date, was reflected in the immediate closure of NATO's ground logistics routes through Pakistan, the eviction of U.S. personnel from the Shamsi airfield in Baluchistan, and a boycott of a December Bonn conference on Afghanistan. At the time of this writing, the supply routes have been closed for more that five months, despite Islamabad's stated intention to allow them to reopen (see "U.S./NATO Ground Lines of Communication" section below).The Pakistani government has rejected U.S. expressions of "deep regret" and "sincere condolences," and demands a formal and unconditional apology from Washington.[47]

The Pentagon quickly launched an investigation in which the Pakistani side refused to participate. That investigation was completed in late December, when the U.S. general heading it announced that, "U.S. forces, given what information they had available to them at the time, acted in self-defense and with appropriate force after being fired upon" and "there was no intentional effort" to target Pakistanis. It was conceded that serious miscommunication and poor coordination were central factors, but no NATO personnel were found to have acted improperly.[48]

Pakistan's military called the "affixing of partial responsibility of the incident on Pakistan ... unjustified and unacceptable." A document detailing the Pakistani perspective was released in January 2012. It conceded that Pakistani forces fired first, but legitimately so in the circumstances. It excoriated the NATO investigators for the "inconceivable" claim that no Pakistani posts were known to be in the area and found the "fundamental cause" of the incident was "the failure of US/ISAF [International Security Assistance Force] to share its near-border

---

[45] Shuja Nawaz, "Who Controls Pakistan's Security Forces?," U.S. Institute of Peace Special Report 297, December 2011; "Pakistan Crisis Shows Army's Limits," Associated Press, January 17, 2012; George Fulton, "Why Pakistan's Zardari Will Not Fall to a Military Coup," *Foreign Affairs* (online), January 22, 2012.

[46] See the November 26, 2011, release at http://www.mofa.gov.pk/mfa/pages/article.aspx?id=1013&type=1.

[47] Expressions of "deepest condolences" came from both Secretary Clinton and Secretary Panetta. See http://islamabad.usembassy.gov/pr-112611b html.

[48] "DOD News Briefing With Brig. Gen. Clark Via Teleconference From Hubert Field, Fla.," Pentagon transcript, December 22, 2011, at http://www.defense.gov/transcripts/transcript.aspx?transcriptid=4952.

operation with Pakistan at any level." It also laid out a timeline suggesting that the incident was "deliberate at some level."[49]

Press reporting indicates the Obama Administration came very close to issuing an apology for Salala on several occasions over ensuing months. Advocates, especially within the State Department, have believed an apology would facilitate a reopening of the GLOCs and a mending of relations more generally. Opponents argued that the United States could not give any appearance of weakness given a compulsion to pressure Pakistan on counterinsurgency. Pentagon figures are said to believe an apology would amount to an admission of fault. In late February, Secretary Clinton reportedly was set to apologize to Foreign Minister Khar in London, but that plan was aborted after U.S. military personnel inadvertently burned Korans in Afghanistan. Later, with coordinated insurgent attacks across Afghanistan in April blamed on the Pakistan-based Haqqani Network, those in the Administration arguing for an apology apparently fell silent.[50]

Notable Developments in 2012

U.S. Congressional Hearing and Legislation on Baluchistan

U.S.-Pakistan relations were further riled in February 2012 when the House Foreign Affairs Subcommittee on Oversight and Investigations held a hearing on Baluchistan, a Pakistani province that is the site of a long-running violent separatist conflict. At least one witness called for the "partition" of Pakistan into substates, Baluchistan among them. Subcommittee Chairman Representative Dana Rohrabacher subsequently offered H.Con.Res. 104 to express the sense of Congress that the people of Baluchistan had a right to self-determination and to their own sovereign country. Although the resolution has only two co-sponsors and has not emerged from committee to date, congressional attention to the issue infuriated the Islamabad government and sparked a storm of criticism from the Pakistani media. Prime Minister Gilani called it an attack on Pakistani sovereignty and Pakistan's Ambassador in Washington warned it "would seriously impact bilateral relations." The Obama Administration distanced itself from the resolution by declaring that it has no policy to support Baluchistan's independence.[51]

Pakistan's Parliamentary Review of the Bilateral Relationship

The Salala incident spurred the Islamabad government to essentially freeze relations with the United States pending a broad review of the engagement by its Parliament. This review, originally slated to be complete in the opening months of 2012, was not finalized until April. Some observers were encouraged by the review process as representing an unusual foreign policy assertiveness by a Pakistani civilian government typically subservient to the military. More cynical analysts saw the review process as merely a civilian face being put upon what is fundamentally a reflection of army policy making. The unanimously approved, 14-point

---

[49] "Pakistan's Perspective on Investigation Report Conducted by BG Stephen Clark Into 26th November 2011 US Led ISAF/NATO Forces Attack on Pakistani Volcano and Boulder Posts in Mohmand Agency," January 23, 2012, at http://www.ispr.gov.pk/front/press/pakistan.pdf.

[50] "U.S. Agonizes Over Apology to Pakistan," *Wall Street Journal*, May 18, 2012.

[51] "Fury in Pakistan After U.S. Congressman Suggests That a Province Leave," *New York Times*, February 22, 2012; Embassy release at http://islamabad.usembassy.gov/pr-021912.html.

"Guidelines for Revised Terms of Engagement with the United States" was issued on April 13, 2012. Among the points/demands most relevant for U.S. policy makers were the following:

- "Immediate cessation of [U.S.-launched] drone attacks inside the territory of Pakistan";

- "Cessation of infiltration into Pakistani territory on any pretext, including 'hot pursuit'";

- "Pakistani territory including its air space shall not be used for transportation of arms and ammunition to Afghanistan";

- "The condemnable and unprovoked NATO/ISAF attack ... represents a breach of international law and constitutes a blatant violation of Pakistan's sovereignty and territorial integrity," and "the government of Pakistan should seek an unconditional apology from the United States";

- "Those held responsible for the [Salala incident] should be brought to justice";

- "No verbal agreement regarding national security shall be entered into by the government" and "all such agreements or understandings shall cease to have effect forthwith";

- "No overt or covert operations inside Pakistan shall be permitted";

- "No private security contractors and/or intelligence operatives shall be allowed"; and

- "Pakistan's territory will not be provided for the establishment of any foreign bases."[52]

The review's authors surprisingly added a request that the United States offer a civil nuclear deal to Pakistan similar to the one offered to India in 2005.

Throughout the review process and following its completion, the Obama Administration has issued repeated and emphatic expressions of respect for Pakistani democracy and sovereignty, even as drone strikes have continued (albeit at a notably reduced rate). U.S. Special Representative for Afghanistan and Pakistan (SRAP) Marc Grossman was in Islamabad in late April for the 6th Trilateral Core Group Meeting of the United States, Pakistan, and Afghanistan. His visit marked the first focused, high-level talks since the Salala incident and included substantive discussion of the Parliament's 14 points. Yet hopes that the bilateral relationship would finally be "reset" and in working order were quickly dashed as Grossman departed without any breakthrough.

Pakistan's demands for a cessation of drone strikes remain a major point of contention—most analysts believe the CIA will be unwilling to relinquish an ability to strike so-called "high-value targets" whenever and wherever the opportunity arises. A continuation of "signature strikes" targeting suspected low-level militants based on "pattern of life" surveillance is also in question. These types of strikes are considered more likely to result in civilian deaths. Some reports suggest that Pakistani leaders will refuse to open NATO's ground supply lines to Afghanistan via the Karachi port until drone strikes are ended, but no government officials have stated this is the case.

---

[52] Pakistan Ministry of Foreign Affairs press release, April 13, 2012.

However, the greater sticking point may be Pakistan's demands for an unconditional apology for the inadvertent deaths of Pakistani soldiers at Salala. At the time of this writing, none of these major issues are resolved and the U.S. government reportedly is withholding at least $1 billion in military reimbursements and counterterrorism funding pending an agreement on bilateral reengagement. Meanwhile, Pakistan's Foreign Ministry continues to insist that Islamabad "will abide by the recommendations of the Parliament both in letter and spirit."[53]

NATO Summit in Chicago

A May 21-22 NATO summit in Chicago—the first ever held in an American city outside of Washington, DC—formally was focused on making decisions about the alliance's future engagement in Afghanistan. Pakistan had boycotted a December 2011 NATO conference in Germany following the Salala incident and it remained unclear for months whether the Islamabad government would be invited to the Chicago meeting, or even participate if invited. Only days before the opening session, President Zardari received a personal call to attend from the NATO Secretary-General. Yet, when the time came, the numerous heads of government in attendance met under the shadow of U.S.-Pakistan tensions and the unresolved GLOCs issue. During the session, President Obama apparently refused to meet in person with President Zardari, a snub that combined with an absence of any apology for Salala to seriously chasten the Pakistanis. Indeed, one unnamed senior U.S. official was quoted as saying there was an intent to make Zardari "feel uncomfortable."[54] Some observers in Pakistan, opposition political figures among them, declared that President Zardari's participation in the summit had been an embarrassment. However, Foreign Minister Khar sounded an upbeat note, arguing that Pakistan was a vital participant and had received an unconditional invitation; Urdu-language editorials were nearly uniform in their (unusual) praise of Zardari for appearing to stand up to international pressure and assert Pakistan's national interests.[55]

Conviction and Sentencing of Doctor Shakil Afridi

On May 23, 2012, a tribal court in northwestern Pakistan convicted Shakil Afridi of treason and sentenced him to 33 years in prison. Afridi, a doctor who had worked with the CIA in an apparently unsuccessful attempt to collect DNA samples from Osama bin Laden's Abbottabad compound previous to the May 2011 U.S. commando raid, had been charged under the colonial-era Frontier Crimes Regulations and was tried outside of the Abbottabad jurisdiction.

The sentence was met with widespread outrage in the United States; the Obama Administration contends there is no reason for Afridi to be held, and the Chairman and Ranking Member of the Senate Armed Services Committee called the sentence "shocking and outrageous," contending that Afridi "should be praised and rewarded for his actions, not punished and slandered." A statement from the Chairman of the Senate Foreign Relations Committee noted the irony that "the only person being punished is the person who helped the United States achieve justice for the murder of thousands of Americans," and concluded that the development will make efforts to

---

[53] Foreign Ministry press release, May 17, 2012.

[54] "U.S.-Pakistan Rift Clouds NATO Summit," *Wall Street Journal*, May 21, 2012.

[55] "NATO Summit: It Was a Very, Very Successful Visit, Says Khar," and "Zardari's Chicago Visit Brought Nothing But Disgrace: Imran," both in *Express Tribune* (Karachi), May 22, 2012.

maintain a strategic relationship more difficult.[56] Islamabad insists the process was in accordance with Pakistani law and should be respected. However, even some Pakistani commentators are questioning the conviction, in particular because he was convicted in a court outside the original jurisdiction, without legal representation, and it is unclear if he has a right to appeal.[57]

Administration Assessments and Bilateral Diplomacy

March 2011 Assessment and FY2011 Certification

The Administration's biannual March 2011 assessment of Afghanistan and Pakistan policy determined that most indicators and metrics against key U.S. objectives had remained static during the reporting period (the latter half of 2010), notably excepting "significant progress" in combating Al Qaeda in the region. On counterinsurgency (COIN) efforts, it noted improved cooperation both within the Pakistani armed forces and between those forces and NATO, but found that the last quarter of 2010 "saw no progress on effectively executing the COIN cycle in KPk [Khyber Pakhtunkhwa province] and the FATA [Federally Administered Tribal Areas]" (see **Figure 2**): "[W]hat remains vexing is the lack of any indication of 'hold' and 'build' planning or staging efforts to compliment ongoing clearing operations. As such, *there remains no clear path toward defeating the insurgency in Pakistan*" [emphasis added].[58]

In apparent conflict with such problematic U.S. government reporting on Pakistan's progress was a March 2011 certification by Secretary Clinton required under Section 203 of the Enhanced Partnership With Pakistan Act of 2009 (P.L. 111-73). This certification, which allowed the release of security-related FY2011 aid to Pakistan, included the Secretary's confirmation that Islamabad was demonstrating "a sustained commitment to and is making significant efforts toward combating terrorist groups" and had "made progress" on ceasing support to extremist and terrorist groups, as well as on preventing Al Qaeda and other terrorist groups from operating on Pakistani territory, and in "dismantling terrorist bases" in the country. In the wake of revelations about Osama bin Laden, and persistent complaints from U.S. military commanders that Pakistan was taking action against the Haqqani Network in the FATA, the certification met with considerable skepticism and appeared driven primarily by political considerations rather than by ground realities. When pressed to further explain the certification at an October 2011 House Foreign Affairs Committee hearing, the Secretary offered, "[A]t the time I made the certification, I closely considered the requirements set forth in the statue and I determined that on balance Pakistan met the legal threshold."[59] To date, there has been no similar certification for FY2012.

---

[56] "Statement By Senators McCain and Levin on Sentencing of Pakistani Doctor Who Assisted in Bin Laden Search," CQ Transcriptions, May 23, 2012; SFRC press release, May 24, 2012.

[57] "Dr Afridi's Conviction: Some Questions" (editorial), *Express Tribune* (Karachi), May 24, 2012.

[58] See "Report on Afghanistan and Pakistan, March 2011" at http://www.fas.org/man/eprint/afpak-0311.pdf.

[59] "Rep. Ileana Ros-Lehtinen Holds Hearing on Afghanistan and Pakistan Transition," CQ Transcriptions, October 27, 2011.

Figure 2. District Map of Pakistan's Khyber Pakhtunkhwa (formally North West Frontier) Province and Federally Administered Tribal Areas

Source: Map Resources. Adapted by CRS.

September 2011 Assessment

The Administration's September 2011 assessment—covering January-June with preliminary comment on July and August—brought little positive news beyond reporting "significant successes" against Al Qaeda, a key aspect of the first of several objectives related to Pakistan: On *enhancing civilian control and stable government in Pakistan,* indicators and metrics "remained static" for the entire reporting period. On *developing Pakistan's COIN capabilities,* indicators and metrics remained static through the first quarter of 2011, then began to decline, with "continued negative trends" into the summer. This was attributed in large degree to the "Pakistan-directed" decrease in bilateral security cooperation. On *involving the international community in efforts to assist in stabilizing Pakistan*, the indicators and metrics were reported to have remained static, with the International Monetary Fund (IMF) Stand-By Arrangement remaining on hold since August 2010 and only limited progress in funding the World Bank Multi-Donor Trust Fund and the U.N. Pakistan Humanitarian Response Plan.[60]

April 2012 Pentagon Report to Congress

The Pentagon's most recent biannual report to Congress on progress toward security and stability in Afghanistan (for the six-month period ending March 31, 2012) noted some positive trends, but flatly stated that, "The Taliban insurgency and its al Qaeda affiliates still operate with impunity from sanctuaries in Pakistan" which "remain the most critical threat" to the U.S.-led effort in Afghanistan. The report contended that the security situation in eastern Afghanistan "remains volatile" and that the city of Kabul continues to face persistent security threats, many of which are "planned in and controlled from Pakistan":

> Pakistan's selective counterinsurgency operations, passive acceptance—and in some cases, provision—of insurgent safe havens, and unwillingness to interdict material such as [improvised explosive device] components, continue to undermine security in Afghanistan and threaten ISAF's campaign.

Pentagon leaders, and U.S. government leaders in general, believe that Pakistan's desire to see an Afghan government "with primacy for the Pashtuns, and limited Indian influence," motivates its leadership to allow insurgent sanctuaries to persist on its soil.[61]

Recent Bilateral Diplomacy

In addition to the several destabilizing developments of 2011 discussed above, U.S.-Pakistan relations have been negatively affected by two other notable issues. One area of contention has been freedom of travel for U.S. diplomats in Pakistan. Incidents in which such diplomats have been prevented from moving between cities reportedly have amounted to "official harassment" from a U.S. perspective, but Pakistani officials insist that requiring "No Objection Certificates" for Americans leaving Islamabad is neither new nor U.S.-specific.[62] Another irritant was the July 2011 revelation that two U.S. citizens of Pakistani origin had for many years been working illicitly on behalf of the ISI in an effort to influence U.S. Kashmir policy.[63]

---

[60] White House Report on Afghanistan and Pakistan, September 2011.

[61] U.S. Department of Defense, "Report on Progress Toward Security and Stability in Afghanistan," April 2012 at http://www.defense.gov/pubs/pdfs/Report_Final_SecDef_04_27_12.pdf.

[62] "American Diplomats in Pakistan Under Pressure," *BBC News*, September 8, 2011.

[63] The men came under federal indictment for failure to register as foreign agents. One of the accused remains at large in Pakistan, but the other, Virginia resident Ghulam Nabi Fai, was arrested for lobbying U.S. lawmakers and funneling campaign contributions to some in Congress over a 10-year period with at least $4 million in funds provided by the ISI. Fai, longtime director of the Kashmiri American Council—a Washington-based nonprofit group ostensibly dedicated to the cause of Kashmir self-determination—admitted to receiving funds from the ISI but insisted his group maintained independence from its viewpoint. The timing of his arrest, coming on the heels of Pakistan's arrest of a doctor charged with aiding the CIA operation against Osama bin Laden, led some to conclude that Washington was sending a message to Islamabad. Fai subsequently pled guilty to conspiracy charges and was sentenced to two years in federal prison.

President Obama has not traveled to Pakistan since taking office, and the bilateral Strategic Dialogue has not had a formal session since October 2010. However, high-level interactions, especially among military and intelligence officials, have continued to be frequent, albeit with a notable late 2011/early 2012 lapse. In October 2011, the Obama Administration made a major show of diplomatic force when Secretary Clinton led a large, high-level delegation to Islamabad. Accompanied by CIA Director David Petraeus, new Joint Chiefs Chairman Gen. Martin Dempsey, Deputy National Security Advisor Lt. Gen. Doug Lute, SRAP Grossman, and other senior officials, Clinton sought to impress upon the entire Pakistani civilian and military leadership that the United States will not tolerate the continued existence of militant safe havens in western Pakistan and will take action against them if the Pakistanis do not.[64]

At the ministerial level, the U.S.-Pakistan Strategic Dialogue appears to have been postponed indefinitely; formal talks including Secretary Clinton, originally slated for March 2011, have not occurred to date. Yet engagement has continued at other levels:

- In February 2012, **Secretary Clinton** met with Foreign Minister Khar in London, where she conveyed U.S. respect for Parliament's right to review bilateral relations and take its time in doing so. Yet the Secretary also conveyed U.S. eagerness to "get back to business," especially on crucial areas such as counterterrorism and Afghanistan. Khar told Clinton that Islamabad needed first to deal with upcoming Senate elections and would soon after deal with Parliament's recommendations.[65]

- In March, **Amb. Grossman** met with President Zardari in Dushanbe, Tajikistan, and emphasized that the United States "wants an honest, constructive, and mutually beneficial relationship with Pakistan and remains committed to continued engagement."[66]

- Days after the Grossman-Zardari meet, **President Obama** sat down with Prime Minister Gilani on the sidelines of a nuclear security summit in Seoul, South Korea, where the President reasserted the U.S. desire to see the two countries "move forward on important shared interests, including counterterrorism and fostering a stable Afghanistan." Like Secretary Clinton, he welcomed Pakistan's parliamentary review process, and also said the United States would welcome Pakistan's potential participation in the upcoming Chicago NATO summit.[67]

- Also in March, senior U.S. and Pakistani military commanders held their first formal talks since the Salala incident when **Central Command chief Gen. James Mattis and NATO-ISAF commander Gen. John Allen** discussed border coordination issues with Gen. Kayani in Rawalpindi.

- In April, **Deputy Secretary of State Thomas Nides** met with Foreign Minister Khar in Islamabad in an effort to build upon the March conversations. Nides

---

[64] "[Clinton] Interview With Nick Schifrin of ABC News," State Department transcript, October 20, 2011; "Clinton Issues Blunt Warning to Pakistan," *New York Times*, October 20, 2011.

[65] "Senior State Department Official on Bilateral Meeting With Secretary Clinton and Foreign Minister Khar of Pakistan," State Department transcript, February 23, 2012.

[66] "Ambassador Grossman's Meeting With President Zardari in Dushanbe," U.S. Embassy release, March 25, 2012.

[67] "Press Briefing by Deputy National Security Advisor for Strategic Communication Ben Rhodes on President Obama's Bilateral Meeting With Prime Minister Gilani of Pakistan," White House transcript, March 27, 2012.

expressed optimism that the two countries could "achieve a balanced approach that respects Pakistan's sovereignty and interests but also represents our concerns about our national security."[68]

- Later in April, **USAID Administrator Rajiv Shah** visited Pakistan to express a strong U.S. commitment to building and improving ties with Pakistan through civilian assistance and development support.[69]

- In late April, **Amb. Grossman** was in Islamabad for the 6th Trilateral Core Group meeting between the United States, Pakistan, and Afghanistan. It was also the first high-level U.S. visit following the release of the parliamentary review. He and interlocutor Foreign Secretary Jalil Abbas Jilani made no breakthroughs on major points of disagreement: Grossman focused on the U.S. desire to see GLOCs quickly reopened, while Jilali reiterated Pakistan's adamant opposition to further drone strikes. By some accounts, it was Washington's refusal to apologize for the Salala incident that ultimately torpedoed the session.[70]

- The U.S.-Pakistan-Afghanistan **Tripartite Commission**—established in 2003 to bring together military commanders for regular discussions on Afghan stability and border security—met for the 35th time in Rawalpindi in mid-May.

Controversy and Furor Over UAV Strikes

Missile strikes in Pakistan reportedly launched by armed American Predator and Reaper unmanned aerial vehicles (UAVs) have been a controversial, but arguably effective tactic against Islamist militants in remote regions of western Pakistan. The nominally covert program is overseen by the CIA, but reports indicate that President Obama personally approves the targeting "kill list."[71] By one assessment, 118 drone strikes occurred in 2010 alone, more than during the preceding six years combined. Seventy more strikes were reported in 2011.[72] The missile strikes in western Pakistan reportedly have taken a significant toll on Al Qaeda and other Islamist extremist militants, but are also criticized as an extrajudicial measure that kills civilians and may also contribute to militant recruitment.

The Pakistani government regularly issues protests over the strikes—and the perception that they violate Pakistani sovereignty fuels considerable anti-American sentiment among the Pakistani public. As per a May 2012 Foreign Ministry statement: "We strongly condemn these drone attacks. We regard them as a violation of our territorial integrity. They are in contravention of international law. They are illegal, counterproductive, and totally unacceptable."[73]

---

[68] "Deputy Secretary Nides: U.S. Supports People of Pakistan," U.S. Embassy transcript, April 4, 2012.

[69] "USAID Administrator Shah: U.S. Committed to Improving U.S.-Pakistan Ties," U.S. Embassy release, April 13, 2012.

[70] "Transcript of the Joint Press Stakeout by Foreign Secretary Jalil Abbas Jilani and Ambassador Marc Grossman," Foreign Ministry release, April 26, 2012; "Lack of a U.S. Apology is Sticking Point for Pakistan," *New York Times* (online), April 30, 2012.

[71] "Secret 'Kill List' Proves a Test of Obama's Principles and Will," *New York Times*, May 29, 2012.

[72] See http://counterterrorism newamerica net/drones.

[73] Foreign Ministry transcript, May 24, 2012.

Still, most observers believe official Pakistan has tacitly allowed the strikes and at times provided intelligence for them.[74] Despite Islamabad's persistent and sweeping rejection of drone strikes on Pakistani territory, informed domestic debate exists, with some analysts welcoming the tactic as necessary and the best of several bad options.[75] There is no shortage of accounts suggesting that, as a tactic, the drone campaign has been effective against Al Qaeda and its FATA-based allies.[76]

Messaging to Pakistan appears to continue to be part of the program's intent: major strikes closely followed both Raymond Davis's March 2011 release and the Administration's July 2011 announcement on partial suspension of U.S. military aid to Islamabad. Most recently, a series of drone strikes came immediately after the May 2012 NATO summit where President Obama refused to meet with his Pakistani counterpart.[77]

Top Administration figures reportedly differ on the wisdom of continuing UAV strikes in Pakistan, with some State Department and Pentagon figures urging the CIA to reduce the pace of its strikes. While there is said to be widespread agreement on the tactical effectiveness of UAV attacks, proponents of their more judicious use reportedly worry that any intense pace aggravates an already troubled relationship with Pakistan and may risk destabilizing that country.[78] A mid-2011 White House review of the program ultimately reaffirmed support for the CIA campaign while also instituting some changes: the State Department would play a greater role in strike decisions, Pakistani officials would get more advanced notice, and strikes would be suspended when Pakistani officials were visiting the United States. the changes appear to have reduced the number of "signature strikes" undertaken against large groups of suspected militants.[79]

In June 2011, the President's top counterterrorism advisor, in referring to the armed drone program, claimed "there hasn't been a single collateral death because of the exceptional proficiency, precision of the capabilities we've been able to develop." Three years after taking office, President Obama publically acknowledged and defended the program's existence, saying it "had not caused a huge number of civilian casualties" and is "kept on a very tight leash."[80] These claims are hotly disputed by independent analysts who track the strikes and estimate that 145-535 civilians have indeed been killed, including scores of children.[81]

---

[74] Leaked U.S. diplomatic cables reportedly describe Army Chief Gen. Kayani as having requested "continuous Predator coverage" over South Waziristan during Pakistan's early 2008 military operations there. The Pakistani military denied having made any requests for armed drone support ("Army Chief Wanted More Drone Support," *Dawn* (Karachi), May 20, 2011).

[75] See, for example, the several related articles in the May 18, 2012, issue of Lahore's *Friday Times*.

[76] See, for example, Pir Zubair Shah, "My Drone War," *Foreign Policy*, March/April 2012.

[77] "Drone Strikes Continue in Pakistan As Tension Increases and Senate Panel Cuts Aid," *New York Times*, May 24, 2012.

[78] "Drone Attacks Split U.S. Officials," *Wall Street Journal*, June 4, 2011.

[79] "Signature strike" decisions are based on "pattern of life" surveillance while "personality strikes" target known leaders. In a March 2012 meeting in London with Lt. Gen. Pasha, CIA Director Petraeus reportedly made a personal offer to refrain from undertaking "signature strikes" and to provide the ISI chief with advanced notice on others, but the concessions apparently were rejected out of hand ("U.S. Tightens Drone Rules," *Wall Street Journal*, November 4, 2011; "Officials: White House Offers to Curtail Drones," Associated Press, March 27, 2012).

[80] John Brennan quoted in "C.I.A. Claim of No Civilian Deaths From Drone Strikes is Disputed," *New York Times*, August 11, 2011; President Obama quoted in "Obama Admits 'Worst-Kept Secret:' US Flies Drones Over Pakistan," *Christian Science Monitor*, January 31, 2012.

[81] "Covert CIA Drones Kill Hundreds of Civilians," *London Sunday Times*, February 5, 2012. An Associated Press assessment found that roughly 70% of those killed by drone strikes are militants, but the New America Foundation finds a success rate of 83% ("New Light on Drone War's Death Toll," Associated Press, February 25, 2012; "CIA (continued...)

Despite the killing of many hundreds of militants and dozens of their commanders, violence in western Pakistan has hardly subsided as a result of missile strikes. Yet, in present circumstances, and with a coming drawdown of NATO troops in neighboring Afghanistan, many commentators believe the U.S. government may have no better option than to continue employing the tactic.

The Inter-Services Intelligence (ISI) Directorate and Bilateral Intelligence Cooperation

Acute Questions About the ISI's Role

Close U.S. links with Pakistan's Inter-Services Intelligence (ISI) date back to the 1980s, when American and Pakistani intelligence officers oversaw cooperative efforts to train and supply Afghan "freedom fighters" who were battling the Soviet Army. Yet mutual mistrust has been ever-present and, in 2008, long-standing doubts about the activities and aims of the ISI compounded. Along with international concerns about the ISI's assumed decades-long strategy of making use of Islamist militant proxies to forward Pakistan's perceived interests, the service is also implicated in extralegal abductions and manipulation of domestic politics.[82]

The agency comes under the direct control of the army and its Director-General, a three-star general, is widely viewed as deputy to the Chief of Army Staff.[83] Lt. Gen. Zaheer-ul-Islam was appointed DG-ISI in March 2012, replacing the retiring Lt. Gen. Pasha. Islam, previously commander of the army's V Corp based in Karachi, received military training in the United States in 2002-2003. Press reports have called him more open and moderate than his predecessors; he may be a candidate for the COAS position after Kayani's scheduled 2012 retirement.[84]

U.S. officials repeatedly have fingered the ISI for actively supporting Afghan insurgents with money, supplies, and planning guidance. There is ongoing conviction among U.S. officials that sanctuaries in Pakistan have allowed Afghan militants to sustain their insurgency and that elements of the ISI continue to support them. Some reporting has cited Afghan insurgent commanders claiming that in the latter months of 2011 the ISI increased its direct contacts with the Taliban, vigorously encouraging more violence, and even supplying them with new high-powered explosives manufactured in Pakistan.[85]

A classified NATO report detailing information gathered through thousands of interrogations of captured Taliban and Al Qaeda militants was leaked in January 2012 and reportedly indicates that

---

(...continued)

Drone War in Pakistan in Sharp Decline," CNN.com, March 27, 2012).

[82] The ISI has come under unprecedented judicial scrutiny related to disappearances and, in 2012, the revival of a 15-year-old vote-rigging scandal involving $6.5 million in alleged covert political donations by the ISI that likely helped unseat Benazir Bhutto's government in 1990 ("Court Challenges Put Unusual Spotlight on Pakistani Spy Agency," *New York Times*, February 7, 2012).

[83] The State Department reports that Pakistan's military and intelligence services nominally report to civilian authorities, but essentially operate without effective civilian oversight (*Country Reports on Human Rights Practices for 2011*, released May 2012).

[84] "Kayani's New Soldier Spy," *India Today* (Delhi), April 2, 2012.

[85] "Afghan Taliban on Night Raids, New Explosives, the ISI, and Peace," *Newsweek*, December 26, 2011.

Afghan insurgents continue to receive direct support from the ISI. The report offers that, "Pakistan's manipulation of the Taliban senior leadership continues unabatedly," and "Senior Taliban leaders meet regularly with ISI personnel, who advise on strategy and relay any pertinent concerns of the government of Pakistan." NATO officials played down the report's significance, and Pakistan's foreign minister called its content "old wine in an even older bottle."[86]

The ISI is also regularly linked to anti-India terrorist groups, including the Lashkar-e-Taiba, responsible for the November 2008 attack on Mumbai in which some 165 people were killed, 6 Americans among them. During a February 2012 House hearing, Secretary of State Clinton asserted, "[T]here is no doubt in my mind that certain elements of the Pakistani government are more ambivalent about cracking down on terrorism. ... [T]here have been relationships between terrorist groups and the military and intelligence services for many decades."[87]

Pakistani officials regularly provide assurances that no elements of the ISI are cooperating with militants or extremists. However, to many independent observers, Pakistan's security services increasingly appear to be penetrated by Islamist extremists.[88] Leaked U.S. diplomatic cables reportedly contained claims that Pakistani military officers receive training biased against the United States.[89] Some analysts argue that, just as Pakistan's national identity has continued to be fractured along the lines dividing nationalism from Islamism, Pakistan's security services can be conceived of as comprising two groups: one, led by Gen. Kayani, is fundamentally nationalist and seeks to maintain the status quo; the other, currently leaderless, is driven by a revisionist Islamist ideology, sometimes with a violent cast.[90]

Even before the Raymond Davis episode began, reports indicated that CIA-ISI relations were at a nadir, with American officials frustrated at the lack of expanded Pakistani military operations and at signs that elements within the ISI continue to provide backing to certain militant groups. The Davis affair sharpened Pakistani attention to—and acrimony toward—the presence of U.S. security officials and contractors in Pakistan. Revelation of Davis's status as a CIA contractor led the ISI to demand an accounting of all such operatives working in Pakistan, but most intelligence cooperation may have been frozen immediately upon the January shooting.[91]

The circumstances of OBL's death brought more focus on purported ISI links with Islamist extremism.[92] Following the May 2011 raid, Pakistan sought to crack down on its own citizens

---

[86] "Pakistan is Helping Afghan Taliban, Says Nato Report," BBC News, January 31, 2012; "Pakistan Denies Claims in NATO Report of Spy Service Still Aiding Taliban," *Washington Post*, February 1, 2012.

[87] "House Foreign Affairs Committee Holds Hearing on President Obama's Fiscal 2013 Budget Proposal for the State Department and Foreign Operations," CQ Transcripts, February 29, 2012.

[88] "Infiltrators Worry Pakistani Military," *Washington Post*, May 28, 2011. In June 2011, a Pakistani brigadier general was arrested and four majors questioned due to their links with the Hizb-ul-Tahrir (Party of Liberation), a nonviolent, but outlawed Islamist group that seeks the establishment of an Islamic caliphate. The general, whose brother may be a senior intelligence officer, is the most senior officer to face such allegations since 1995 ("Arrest of Pakistani Officer Revives Fears of Extremism Within Military," CNN.com, June 22, 2011).

[89] "Anti-Americanism Rife in Pakistan Army Institution – Wikileaks," Reuters, May 25, 2011.

[90] Pervez Hoodbhoy, "Pakistan's Army: Divided It Stands," Viewpoint Online (undated), at http://www.viewpointonline.net/pakistans-army-divided-it-stands.html.

[91] "U.S.-Pakistan Intelligence Operations Frozen Since January," Reuters, April 9, 2011.

[92] The mobile phone of bin Laden's most trusted courier reportedly contained contacts in the Harakat-ul-Mujahideen, a Kashmir-oriented terrorist group with close ties to the ISI and deep roots in the Abbottabad area. Its leader, Maulana Fazlur Rehman Khalil, a sometime ally of OBL, continues to live openly in Islamabad ("Seized Phone Offers Clues to Bin Laden's Pakistani Links," *New York Times*, June 24, 2011).

---

who were found to be working with the CIA.[93] Pressure was increased to allow American investigators access to bin Laden's three widows in Pakistani custody. Such access was subsequently granted. One week after OBL's death, a Pakistani newspaper seen as close to the country's military and intelligence services published the purported name of the CIA's Islamabad station chief. This was the second time in six months that the top covert American operative in Pakistan had been outed, and U.S. officials reportedly believed such disclosures were deliberate as a means for the ISI to demonstrate its leverage and to express anger at U.S. policies.[94]

After the OBL raid, the ISI leadership was confronted more frequently—and more publically— with U.S. evidence of collusion between Pakistani officials and Afghan insurgents. Such evidence notably included instances in which the CIA alerted Islamabad about the existence of two bomb-making facilities in Pakistan's Federally Administered Tribal Areas (FATA), only to have Pakistani army units find the sites abandoned by the time they arrived. This led U.S. officials to assume that the targets had been tipped off about upcoming raids, a charge called "totally false and malicious" by the Pakistani military, which declared that some of the intelligence provided "proved to be incorrect." Still, U.S. officials repeated the accusations after militants fled two other bomb-making facilities; these officials reportedly believed that Pakistan's insistence on gaining permission from local tribal elders before entering the area allowed militants to escape.[95]

Continuing Intelligence Cooperation

Concurrent with interagency discord, effective joint intelligence work has continued. Just days after the OBL raid, a Yemeni national described as a "senior" or "midlevel" Al Qaeda operative was arrested in Karachi with the help of U.S.-provided intelligence. Mohammed Ali Qasim Yaqub reportedly had been a key courier between Al Qaeda's top leaders, and his capture was seen as a good-faith Pakistani effort to mend relations with Washington. In another apparent effort to rebuild confidence, Pakistan pledged in June to grant more than three dozen visas to CIA officers. Most-wanted terrorist Ilyas Kashmiri was reported killed in a June 2011 drone strike in South Waziristan, and the new Al Qaeda chief's deputy and operational commander, Libyan explosives expert Atiyah Abd al-Rahman, was reported killed in an August strike in North Waziristan (successes in targeting militants in the FATA with unmanned drones likely come with intelligence from Pakistan). In September, Pakistan announced having arrested three allegedly senior Al Qaeda operatives near Quetta with help from technical assistance provided by the CIA.

Bilateral intelligence cooperation, especially that targeting Al Qaeda and the "Pakistani Taliban," has quietly continued even as government-to-government relations have worsened.[96] Some reports indicate that the CIA has undertaken a years-long, multibillion dollar effort to establish inside Pakistan a network of "secret friends" of the United States—security officials, intelligence

---

[93] "Arrest Indicates Pakistan Leaders Face Rising Pressure to Curb U.S. Role," *Washington Post*, June 15, 2011.

[94] "Pakistanis Disclose Name of CIA Operative," *Washington Post*, May 9, 2011.

[95] "C.I.A. Director Warns Pakistan on Collusion With Militants," *New York Times*, June 12, 2011, ISPR press release, June 17, 2011; "Pakistan Still Tipping Off Militants, U.S. Officials Say," *Los Angeles Times*, June 19, 2011.

[96] For example, drone strikes were temporarily halted after the November 2011 Salala border incident, by some accounts providing respite to FATA-based militants. However—and despite Islamabad's official opposition—they resumed with a mid-January strike that reportedly killed a senior Al Qaeda figure. That attack was taken as evidence that Pakistanis were at some level continuing to assist in targeting ("How Pakistan Helps the U.S. Drone Campaign," Reuters, January 22, 2012).

operatives, counterterrorism fighters, and the like, who could offer an alternative to less trustworthy army and ISI officials.[97]

Pakistan and the Afghan Insurgency[98]

Pakistani leaders have long sought access to Central Asia and "strategic depth" with regard to India through friendly relations with neighboring Afghanistan. Such policy contributed to President-General Zia ul-Haq's support for Afghan mujahideen "freedom fighters" who were battling Soviet invaders during the 1980s and to Islamabad's later support for the Afghan Taliban regime from 1996 to 2001.[99] British colonialists had purposely divided the ethnic Pashtun tribes inhabiting the mountainous northwestern reaches of their South Asian empire with the 1893 "Durand Line." This porous, 1,600-mile border is not accepted by Afghan leaders, who have at times fanned Pashtun nationalism to the dismay of Pakistanis.[100] Both Pakistan and Afghanistan play central roles as U.S. allies in global efforts to combat Islamic militancy. Ongoing acrimony between Islamabad and Kabul is thus deleterious to U.S. interests.

American and Pakistani goals in Afghanistan are far from fully compatible; there is very little agreement beyond the shared interest in a negotiated settlement that leaves Afghanistan relatively stable and secure. Pakistan—and especially its military and intelligence services—is widely believed to be seeking a post-NATO Afghanistan that is deferential to and perhaps even dependent upon Islamabad, with Kabul setting foreign policies that do not run counter to Pakistani interests. In contrast, the U.S.-led coalition endeavors to leave behind a capable and independent Afghanistan. Such a result would almost certainly see the Kabul government increase its cooperation with India. If within this dynamic Pakistan makes use of the Quetta Shura and Haqqani Network as proxies in its dealings with Kabul (as is widely assumed to have been the case for several years now), the Administration's continued reliance on Islamabad in creating and shaping the reconciliation process is likely to increase Pakistan's leverage.[101]

Washington has continued to seek Islamabad's support for Afghan reconciliation talks, ideally by winning ISI pressure on Afghan insurgency leaders to negotiate. Yet tensions between the two governments' respective approaches are evident in the fact that Americans want to "fight, talk,

---

[97] See Eli Lake, "America's Shadow State in Pakistan," The DailyBeast.com, December 5, 2011.

[98] See also CRS Report RL30588, *Afghanistan: Post-Taliban Governance, Security, and U.S. Policy*, by Kenneth Katzman.

[99] Documentary evidence indicates that Islamabad provided military and economic support, perhaps including the combat troops, to the Afghan Taliban during the latter half of the 1990s (see "Pakistan: 'The Taliban's Godfather'?," National Security Archive Briefing Book 227, August 14, 2007).

[100] Pakistan is home to more than 30 million Pashto-speaking people, most of them living near the border with Afghanistan, which is home to perhaps 15 million ethnic Pashtuns (also known as Pakhtuns or Pathans). A hardy people with a proud martial history (they are disproportionately represented in the Pakistani military), Pashtuns played an important role in the anti-Soviet resistance of the 1980s.

[101] See Ashley Tellis, "Gambling on Reconciliation to Save a Transition: Perils and Possibilities in Afghanistan," Carnegie Endowment for International Peace Policy Outlook, December 2011. Many analysts contend that American and Pakistan objectives in Afghanistan are "fundamentally at odds," meaning a U.S. reliance on Pakistan to forge Afghan reconciliation is a "dangerous gamble" given the apparent failure of a "decade-long policy of seeking to appease Pakistan and induce its cooperation through large-scale economic and military assistance (first two quotes from Ashley Tellis, third from Christine Fair, in "Rep. Steve Chabot Holds a Hearing on U.S. Policy Toward Afghanistan and Pakistan," CQ Transcripts, November 3, 2011. For a detailed argument of why "Pakistan is the problem," see Tellis's prepared statement at http://foreignaffairs.house.gov/112/tel110311.pdf).

build," while Pakistanis are seen to be taking a "cease-fire, talk, wait for the Americans to leave" tack. Pakistani officials have been confused by a perceived lack of clarity in U.S. goals for Afghanistan and in pressure from Washington to employ force against anti-Kabul militants in North Waziristan even as the U.S. government seeks to talk with other insurgent groups.[102] Some argue that Washington risks rewarding Pakistani intransigence by giving that country's security services a key role in brokering peace with the same insurgent forces they have fostered. Some even contend that the ISI has spent the past decade trying to reinstate the Taliban regime overthrown by the ISAF coalition in 2001.[103]

Ongoing Turmoil in Pakistan-Afghanistan Relations

Senior U.S. officials and nearly all independent observers continue to contend that Pakistani cooperation is necessary for reconciliation and long-term stability in Afghanistan. Islamabad's relations with Kabul remain troubled, and it is widely understood that Afghan insurgents continue to find safe havens in the Pakistani cities of Quetta and Karachi, as well as in western Pakistan's tribal agencies. U.S. military commanders identify these havens as central obstacles to successful pacification of southern and eastern Afghanistan. Declassified U.S. government documents indicate that the Taliban's resurgence in the mid-2000s could not have been possible in the absence of FATA sanctuaries.[104]

Despite some warming of Pakistan-Afghanistan ties in 2010 and early 2011, Afghan officials continue to openly accuse Pakistan of aiding and abetting terrorism inside Afghanistan. There are signs that Afghan's historic wariness of Pakistani influence in their country is not abating.[105] Many analysts have grown cynical given perceptions of Islamabad's consistent use of "Pashtun jihadi proxies" to forward its perceived interests and the Pakistani military's aim to exert dominance of its Afghan neighbors.[106]

Islamabad can be discomfited by signs that the U.S. presence in Afghanistan is not long-term or that the international community may "abandon" the region in ways damaging to Pakistani interests, as was the case during the 1990s.[107] Many analysts saw President Obama's June 2011 announcement of an impending U.S. military drawdown from Afghanistan as yet another signal to stakeholder governments and Taliban elements, alike, that the U.S. focus is on an exit strategy and that the United States may not make a long-term commitment to stabilizing the region.

---

[102] "U.S. Seeks Aid From Pakistan in Peace Effort," *New York Times*, October 31, 2011.

[103] See, for example, Sarah Chayes, "Denying Pakistan" (op-ed), *Los Angeles Times*, November 23, 2011.

[104] "'No-Go' Tribal Areas Became Basis for Afghanistan Insurgency, Documents Show," National Security Archive Electronic Briefing Book No. 325, posted September 13, 2010.

[105] See, for example, "Ordinary Afghans Voicing Increasing Distrust of Pakistan's Intentions," Radio Free Europe/Radio Liberty (online), November 6, 2011.

[106] "Talking About Talks: Toward Political Settlement in Afghanistan," International Crisis Group Asia Report No. 221, March 20, 2012.

[107] Members of Pakistan's nongovernmental foreign policy "elite" are reported to maintain that Pakistan's key objective is to see a pacific Afghanistan with an inclusive government and a limited Indian presence, even in the area of economic and social development. From this perspective, only significant power-sharing with Afghan Pashtuns will ensure a future Kabul government sensitive to Pakistani interests, (see Moeed Yusuf, Huma Yusuf, and Salman Zaidi, "Pakistan, the United States, and the End Game in Afghanistan: Perceptions of Pakistan's Foreign Policy Elite," U.S. Institute of Peace, July 25, 2011).

Pakistani leaders insist that Afghan stability is a vital Pakistani interest. In April 2011, Prime Minister Gilani, Army Chief Kayani, and ISI Director Pasha all traveled to Kabul as part of an effort to upgrade the Afghanistan-Pakistan Joint Commission earlier that year and so accelerate the peace process. American observers were disturbed by reports that Gilani had used the meetings as an opportunity to wean Kabul away from its strategic partnership with the United States, and instead move closer to Islamabad and seek greater support from China. According to the reports, Gilani criticized America's "imperial designs" and contended that ending the Afghan war required Kabul and Islamabad to take "ownership" of the peace process.[108] The new Joint Commission met in June 2011, with Gilani and President Karzai expressing their commitment to an "Afghan-led and Afghan-owned" process. The two sides also produced a 23-point "Islamabad Declaration" pledging improved and deepened ties in a wide range of issue-areas.[109]

However, in the summer of 2011, increased incidence of "reverse infiltration" caused friction between Islamabad and Kabul, especially after more than two dozen Pakistani soldiers were killed in a June cross-border raid by up to 400 militants from Afghanistan's Kunar province. Later that month Afghan officials accused Pakistan of firing more than 760 rockets into the Kunar, Nangarhar, and Khost provinces over a period of six weeks, killing at least 60 people, including women and children. Pakistan rejected charges that its forces had been involved in any cross-border attacks. Some in Afghanistan see the barrages as part of an orchestrated and official Pakistani effort to "reshape Afghanistan as a Pakistani colony" after International Security Assistance Force (ISAF) troops draw down.[110]

Pakistan-Afghanistan relations reached a new nadir in September 2011 when Afghan High Peace Council chairman and former Afghan President Burhanuddin Rabbani was assassinated in his Kabul home by a suicide bomber, dealing a major blow to hopes for reconciliation talks. Afghan officials suspect the ISI played a role in the murder, saying the attacker was Pakistani and the attack had been planned in Quetta. They also criticized Islamabad for its alleged failure to cooperate in the related investigation. Pakistani officials denied playing any part in the assassination, but the Afghan president has continued to accuse Pakistan of "using terrorism" as official policy. In October, Afghan intelligence officials claimed to have halted a plot to assassinate Karzai himself and said the alleged culprits were based in the FATA and affiliated with both Al Qaeda and the Haqqanis.[111]

Afghan Reconciliation and Pakistan's Role

Islamabad strongly endorses current efforts to make peace with the Afghan Taliban and insists that the parameters for such a process should be set by the Kabul government. Pakistan considers itself to be indispensible to successful Afghan peace talks, and Islamabad's leaders are in large part motivated by a desire to deny India significant influence in a post-conflict Afghanistan. Pakistan has sought to exert control over which Taliban figures can negotiate on this account. In early 2010, the Afghan Taliban's top military commander and key aide to Mullah Omar, Mullah

---

[108] "Karzai Told to Dump U.S.-Pakistan Urges Afghanistan to Ally With Islamabad, Beijing," *Wall Street Journal*, April 27, 2011.

[109] See the June 12, 2011, text at http://www.mofa.gov.pk/Press_Releases/2011/June/Pr_200 htm.

[110] "Pakistan Launching Military Intervention to Subjugate Afghanistan," MEMRI Inquiry & Analysis Series Report No. 703, July 6, 2011.

[111] "Karzai Says Pakistan is Supporting Terrorists," *Washington Post*, October 4, 2011; "Afghans Say Plot Aimed to Kill Karzai," *Los Angeles Times*, October 6, 2011.

Abdul Ghani Baradar, was captured in a joint ISI-CIA operation in Karachi. By some accounts, Pakistani elements "orchestrated" the Baradar arrest to facilitate talks with "willing" Taliban commanders and pave the way for reconciliation negotiations. Cynics contend that the ISI's motives may simply have been to thwart any anticipated negotiations.

In mid-2010, Pakistan launched an effort to broker a reconciliation between the Kabul government and the Haqqani Network. This initiative sparked concerns that Islamabad would seek to exploit the political situation—both in the region and in Washington—to mold a settlement giving Pakistan maximal influence in a post-conflict Kabul. Later that year NATO facilitated the secret travel of at least three QST figures and a representative of the Haqqani Network from Pakistan to Kabul for meetings with senior Afghan government officials. It is unclear whether Pakistani officials were included in this process; some reports indicated they were not, others described ISI officials as having participated directly.

In another clear indication that Islamabad has substantive influence over top Afghan insurgents, in the fall of 2011 the U.S. Ambassador to Afghanistan suggested that Pakistan is hesitant to allow Taliban leaders to travel to Kabul for reconciliation talks. He asks that Pakistan support the process by allowing those willing to talk to be given the opportunity to do so. Afghan President Karzai has echoed these complaints, saying insurgent leaders inside Pakistan are not sufficiently independent of Pakistani control to enter into negotiations on their own.[112]

By early 2012, the Islamabad government appeared to at least be allowing the U.S.-Taliban negotiating initiative to proceed. Then, on an April visit to Islamabad, Afghan President Karzai reportedly asked Pakistani leaders to "use their influence" to prod the Taliban into negotiations, a request that Foreign Minister Khar called "not only unrealistic, but preposterous." Yet, just a week later, Prime Minister Gilani issued an unprecedented open appeal to the Afghan Taliban leadership and other militant commanders to "participate in an intra-Afghan process for national reconciliation and peace."[113] The Obama Administration welcomed the message, even as there remain pervasive concerns that Pakistan's security services are maintaining ties with and possibly supporting certain Afghan insurgent groups as a means of increasing their leverage in the reconciliation process. To many observers in Pakistan and the region more widely, current U.S. transition planning for Afghanistan appears to be cover for a hasty exit strategy.

Haqqani Network Attacks and U.S. Frustrations

The terrorist network led by Jalaluddin Haqqani and his son Sirajuddin, based in the FATA, is commonly identified as the most dangerous of Afghan insurgent groups battling U.S.-led forces in eastern Afghanistan. In the words of one expert,

> The Haqqani Network represents a strategic threat to the enduring stability of the Afghan state and U.S. national security interests in the region. The Haqqanis are currently Afghanistan's most capable and potent insurgent group, and they continue to maintain close operational and strategic ties with al-Qaeda and their affiliates.

---

[112] "Envoy: Pakistan Should Aid Talks," *USA Today*, September 8, 2011; "Karzai Lashes Out at Pakistan," *Financial Times* (London), October 3, 2011.

[113] "Meeting in Pakistan Reveals Tensions Over Afghan Talks," *New York Times*, February 18, 2012; "Statement of Prime Minister Syed Yusuf Gilani on Afghanistan," Foreign Ministry transcript, February 24, 2012.

This analyst is among many who contend that the group is not reconcilable and must be dealt with through sustained military offensives by ISAF and Afghan forces beyond 2012.[114]

Islamabad officials have consistently deferred on urgent and long-standing U.S. requests that the Pakistani military launch operations against the Haqqanis' North Waziristan haven, saying their forces are already stretched too thin. Most observers believe the underlying cause of Pakistan's inaction is the country's decades-long relationship with Jalaluddin Haqqani and a belief held in the army and ISI that his group represents perhaps the best chance for Islamabad to exert Pashtun-based influence in post-ISAF Afghanistan.

Over the past year, the Haqqanis have undertaken numerous high-visibility attacks in Afghanistan that infuriated top U.S. and Afghan officials. First, a June 2011 assault on Kabul's Intercontinental Hotel by Haqqani gunmen and suicide bombers left 18 people dead. Then, in September, a truck bomb attack on a U.S. military base by Haqqani fighters in the Wardak province injured 77 American troops and killed 5 Afghans. But it was a September 13, 2011, attack on the U.S. Embassy compound in Kabul that appears to have substantively changed the nature of U.S.-Pakistan relations, a well-planned and -executed 20-hour-long assault that left 16 Afghans dead, 5 police officers and at least 6 children among them. Although U.S. officials dismissed the attack as a sign of the insurgents' weakness, the ability of militants to undertake a complex raid in the heart of Kabul's most protected area was seen by many as a clear blow to the narrative of Afghanistan becoming more secure.

Days after this attack, Admiral Mullen called on General Kayani to again press for Pakistani military action against Haqqani bases. Apparently unsatisfied with his counterpart's response, Mullen returned to Washington, D.C., and began ramping up rhetorical pressure to previously unseen levels, accusing the ISI of using the Haqqanis to conduct a "proxy war" in Afghanistan. Meanwhile, Secretary Panetta issued what was taken by many to be an ultimatum to Pakistan when he told reporters that the United States would "take whatever steps are necessary to protect our forces" in Afghanistan from future attacks by the Haqqanis.[115] Then, during September 22 testimony before the Senate Armed Services Committee, Mullen issued the strongest and most direct U.S. government statement on Pakistani malfeasance of the post-2001 era, saying,

> *The Haqqani network, for one, acts as a veritable arm of Pakistan's Inter-Services Intelligence agency.* With ISI support, Haqqani operatives plan and conducted that [September 13] truck bomb attack, as well as the assault on our embassy. We also have credible evidence they were behind the June 28th attack on the Intercontinental Hotel in Kabul and a host of other smaller but effective operations. [emphasis added][116]

---

[114] Jeffrey Dressler, "The Haqqani Network: A Strategic Threat," Institute for the Study of War Middle East Security Report 9, March 2012. Another overview describes the network as interdependent with Al Qaeda, an enabler for other jihadi groups, and "the fountainhead of local, regional, and global militancy." It is also called the "primary conduit" for Pakistani Taliban fighters to transit into Afghanistan and as the "central diplomatic interface" between the TTP and the Pakistani government. The report is pessimistic on the network's potential to disengage itself from Al Qaeda (Dan Rassler and Vahid Brown, "The Haqqani Nexus and the Evolution of Al-Qa'ida," Combating Terrorism Center at West Point Harmony Program, July 13, 2011).

[115] "Joint Chiefs Chairman Presses Pakistan on Militant Havens," *New York Times*, September 17, 2011; U.S. Says Pakistani Spies Using Group for 'Proxy War,'" Reuters, September 21, 2011; "U.S. Issues Sharp Warning on Militant Ties," *Washington Post*, September 21, 2011.

[116] "Senate Armed Services Committee Holds Hearing on Iraq and Afghanistan," CQ Transcripts, September 22, 2011. Recently retired Defense Secretary Robert Gates later offered, "There's little question in my mind that [the Haqqanis] receive support and protection from the ISI." Mullen's strong language may have come as a result of his (continued...)

Secretary Panetta, testifying alongside Mullen, took the opportunity to add, "I think the first order of business right now is to, frankly, put as much pressure on Pakistan as we can to deal with this issue from their side."[117] The statements of America's two top military officials were widely seen to signal a new and more strident level of U.S. intolerance for Pakistan's regional "double-game."

Publically, the Obama Administration did not fully align itself with Admiral Mullen's charges. President Obama himself later stated, "I think the intelligence is not as clear as we might like in terms of what exactly the [ISI-Haqqani] relationship is," but he still insisted that the Pakistanis "have got to take care of this problem" in any case."[118] Later reporting called the Wardak truck bombing a "turning point" in hardening Secretary Clinton's attitude toward the Haqqanis.[119] In ensuing months, Haqqani fighters have been implicated in numerous further attacks on coalition targets in Afghanistan, including coordinated, country-wide attacks launched in mid-April, 2012.

Islamabad rejects claims that Pakistan is responsible for spates of violence in Afghanistan or that it supports or has control over the Haqqanis. The Pakistani military called Mullen's statements "very unfortunate and not based on fact," and categorically denied conducting a proxy war or supporting the Haqqanis. A stern Foreign Minister Khar warned that, with such allegations, the United States could "lose an ally." President Zardari, in an op-ed response, said that "verbal assaults" against Pakistan are damaging the bilateral relationship"[120]

A Haqqani Role in Afghan Reconciliation or FTO Designation?

As noted above, Pakistani officials have for nearly two years sought to facilitate a rapprochement between the Haqqanis and the Kabul government, but close Haqqani links with Al Qaeda have been a major sticking point (Al Qaeda figures are widely believed to enjoy sanctuary in Haqqani-controlled areas). Pakistan—especially through its military and intelligence agencies—is seen to wield considerable clout with the Haqqanis and may be the only actor able to prod them toward negotiations. Unnamed Pakistani military officials have claimed they can "deliver" the Haqqanis to a negotiating table and that this is the only viable policy option (on the assumption that a military assault on Haqqani bases would only engulf the region in a conflict the Pakistani military would likely be unable to win). However, by bringing the insurgent group into negotiations, Islamabad would be guaranteed a central role in the ensuing process, a development some in Washington and other interested capitals wish to avoid.

The Obama Administration has been considering formally designating the Haqqani Network as a Foreign Terrorist Organization (FTO) under U.S. law, especially with pressure to do so coming from some senior Senators, Armed Services Committee Chairman Senator Carl Levin and Intelligence Committee Co-Chair Senator Dianne Feinstein among them.[121] Seven Haqqani

---

(...continued)

disappointment that a planned Pakistani offensive against the Haqqanis—reportedly worked out between himself and Kayani earlier this year—did not materialize ("Gates: Pakistan Spy Agency Tied to Militant Group," *Wall Street Journal*, October 6, 2011; "How Pakistan Lost Its Top U.S. Friend," *Wall Street Journal*, September 28, 2011).

[117] "Senate Armed Services Committee Holds Hearing on Iraq and Afghanistan," CQ Transcripts, September 22, 2011.

[118] Quoted in "Obama: Pakistan Must Sort Out Haqqani 'Problem,'" Agence France Presse, September 30, 2011.

[119] "Top US Delegation to Enlist Pakistan's Help," Associated Press, October 19, 2011.

[120] ISPR press release, September 23, 2011; "Pakistan Warns US It Could 'Lose an Ally,'" *Financial Times* (London), September 23, 2011; Asif Ali Zardari, "Talk To, Not At, Pakistan" (op-ed), *Washington Post*, October 2, 2011.

[121] "US Weighs Blacklisting Haqqani Network," Agence France Presse, September 26, 2011.

---

leaders have been under U.S. sanctions since 2008 and, in 2011, Secretary Clinton designated operational commander Badruddin Haqqani under Executive Order 13224. However, the potential decision on an FTO designation is complicated by the Administration's apparent willingness to negotiate with the Haqqani leadership, something that has occurred at least once in the recent past (without result), and that Secretary Clinton has indicated may be necessary again in order to establish sustainable peace in Afghanistan. The Haqqani Network Terrorist Designation Act of 2011 (S. 1959) was passed out of the Senate by unanimous consent in December 2011, but has not emerged from House committee to date. U.S. congressional frustration with the Administration's now overdue "formal review" on the question of FTO designation has only increased in 2012.[122]

Pakistan and Improvised Explosive Devices (IEDs) in Afghanistan

Ammonium nitrate (AN) is widely used fertilizer that also has commercial uses as a chemical explosives precursor. The great majority of improvised explosive devices (IEDs) used by Islamist insurgents fighting in Afghanistan employ AN and, since the Kabul government's January 2010 ban on the substance, nearly all illicit AN in Afghanistan is believed to arrive via transshipments from neighboring Pakistan.[123] According to data from the Pentagon's Joint Improvised Explosive Device Defeat Organization (JIEDDO), the summer of 2011 saw historic peaks in total IED "events" in Afghanistan. However, with improved detection and clearing capabilities—and a major increase in cache finds—the "effective" IED attack rate has declined.[124] Section 503 of the Intelligence Authorization Act of FY2012 (became P.L. 112-87 in January 2012) required the Director of National Intelligence and Secretary of Defense to submit to Congress a report on a coordinated strategy for countering IED-related networks in both Pakistan and Afghanistan. This reporting requirement would be renewed by pending FY2103 legislation.

The U.S. government is urging Islamabad to adjust Pakistani national laws to restrict access to AN there or, short of that, to encourage Pakistani law enforcement and border security agencies to be more active and effective in efforts to prevent its movement into Afghanistan. Washington's relevant efforts fall into three main categories: (1) diplomatic initiatives; (2) law enforcement initiatives; and (3) science and technology efforts. JIEDDO, the State Department's SRAP staff, and staff of the Department of Homeland Security's Immigration and Customs Enforcement office are engaged in these efforts. In addition, Operation Global Shield (also known as Project Global Shield) is an unprecedented multilateral law enforcement operation launched in late 2010 to combat the illicit cross-border diversion and trafficking of 11 chemical explosives precursors (including AN) by monitoring their cross-border movements. A U.S.-proposed collaborative effort of the World Customs Organization, the U.N. Office on Drugs and Crime, and Interpol, the program has realized some notable successes to date.[125] Adding urea fertilizer granules to AN can

---

[122] "US Secretly Met Afghan Militants," *Wall Street Journal*, October 5, 2011; "U.S. Open to Afghan Peace Deal Including Haqqani," Reuters, October 11, 2011; "U.S. Lawmakers Want Pakistan Network to be Dubbed Terrorists," *Los Angeles Times*, May 11, 2012.

[123] Pentagon officials have said that 85% of Afghan IEDs use AN manufactured in Pakistan ("Tensions With Pakistan Rise Over Bomb Ingredient," *National Journal Daily*, July 6, 2011).

[124] Author interview with JIEDDO official, August 4, 2011.

[125] Since 2010, 89 participating nations and international organizations have been sharing information about the export of 14 precursor chemicals used IEDs. As of January 2012, Program Global Shield had accounted for seizures of chemical precursors totaling over 62 metric tons and 31 arrests related to the illicit diversion of these chemicals. (Homeland Security Department release, January 25, 2012; see also http://m.ice.gov/news/releases/1111/111121washingtondc htm).

make processing the mixture for explosives more complicated and is recommended by experts. Other options include adding colored dyes to the AN fertilizer to make it easier to spot at checkpoints or adding radio frequency identification tags so as to track AN shipments.[126]

Pakarab Fertilizers Ltd., in the central Pakistani city of Multan, is the country's largest fertilizer complex and has been in operation since 1979 (it was privatized in 2005). As reported by the Pakistani Ministry of Industries and Production, the Multan facility has produced well over 300,000 metric tons of AN annually since 2004.[127] There is pending legislation in Islamabad that would adjust relevant Pakistani national laws to further restrict AN and other precursors. However, this "Explosives Ordinance" has remained in draft stage only, meaning that near-term changes are unlikely. The Islamabad government has established a National Counter-IED Forum in which all relevant Pakistani agencies can work together to develop an action plan. In the absence of an outright ban, the United States has had to rely on Pakistani police and border authorities who are vulnerable to corruption.

U.S./NATO Ground Lines of Communication

NATO has been dependent upon ground and air lines of communication (GLOCs and ALOCs) through and over Pakistan to supply its forces in landlocked Afghanistan. To date, the logistics routes used by NATO to supply the Afghanistan effort have been closed for six months as a result of Pakistan's anger over the Salala incident and broader pique about the state of its relationship with Washington. The surface routes had regularly come under attack by militants, and were temporarily closed in the past in apparent efforts to convey Islamabad's leverage. In 2008, insurgents began more focused attempts to interdict these supply lines, especially near the historic Khyber Pass connecting Peshawar with Jalalabad, Afghanistan, but also to include the route from Karachi to Kandahar, which runs through Quetta and the Chaman border crossing. Such efforts left thousands of transport and fuel trucks destroyed, and numerous Pakistani drivers dead. To reach the Afghan border from Karachi, truck drivers typically must pay bribes to police and other government officials, and in some instances the trucks destroyed en route have first been emptied of their fuel and other cargo, which can end up for sale at Peshawar markets.[128]

In response to interdiction attacks and to reduce reliance on Pakistan, the U.S. military began testing alternative routes, concentrating especially on lines from Central Asia and Russia. By mid-2010, this "Northern Distribution Network" (NDN) was carrying well over half of NATO's total supplies, but only "nonlethal" cargo moves via the NDN. While senior U.S. defense officials prefer Pakistan as a faster and less expensive logistics route, they have continued to expand aerial and NDN routes, even if the former is up to ten times as costly and the latter entails greater U.S. reliance on authoritarian regimes in Central Asia.

Loss of the Pakistani GLOCs has proven to be less damaging to Afghan operations than many expected. In early May, the British deputy commander of ISAF forces said they were "managing very well" without the Pakistani GLOCs, but that reopening them would by "extremely helpful" and also provide financial benefits to Pakistanis. Later in the month, Gen. Allen offered that closure of the GLOCs "has not, in fact, negatively affected ... our prosecution of the

---

[126] "To Stop Afghan Bombs, A Focus On Pakistani Fertilizer," *Washington Post*, November 25, 2011.

[127] See http://www.moip.gov.pk/fertilizerProduction htm.

[128] "Route of Death: Nato Supply Tankers Bribe Their Way to the Border," *Express Tribune* (Karachi), July 11, 2011.

campaign."[129] However, the Pentagon's April report on Afghanistan and Pakistan called the continued closure of the GLOCs a "strategic concern" that has hampered Afghan security forces by backlogging thousands of tons of equipment for them. It counted more than 4,100 vehicles "stranded" in Pakistan due to the closure while noting that airlift capabilities have limited the closure's effect on the movement of communications equipment and weapons. In withdrawing from Afghanistan, NATO will need to remove at least 100,000 thousand shipping containers and 70,000 vehicles worth at least $30 billion.[130]

As the spring "fighting season" in Afghanistan approached in early 2012, U.S. commanders became more insistent about the need to have Pakistani GLOCs reopened. In mid-March, all major Pakistani political and military principles met and agreed "in principle" to reopen the GLOCs and, as noted above, the Pakistani parliamentary review finalized in mid-April called for same. By mid-May, senior Pakistani officials were indicating that reopening was imminent: Foreign Minister Khar offered that, "Pakistan has made a point and now we can move on."[131]

Statements from both governments suggested a deal had already been struck well before the Chicago summit, with one report saying Islamabad was seeking a fee of $1,500-1,800 per truck. Yet—only days before the Chicago summit—Pakistani negotiators reportedly proposed a fee of $5,000 per truck, which would represent a 20-fold increase from previous levels. Such a drastic price hike is seen to be especially hard for the Pentagon to accept, given that for many years use of Pakistani GLOCs was considered to be "free" in exchange for billion of dollars in CSF reimbursements paid to Islamabad.[132] The Chairman and Ranking Member of the Senate Armed Services Committee said the $5,000 fee was unacceptable; the latter Member reportedly called it "extortion."[133] To date, negotiations on the issue have not reached a resolution.

Indigenous Islamist Militancy and Pakistani Military Operations

Indigenous Militancy

Islamist extremism and militancy has been a menace to Pakistani society throughout the post-2001 period, becoming especially prevalent since 2007, but the rate of attacks and number of victims may have peaked in 2009. In addition to widespread Islamist violence, Pakistan currently suffers from a serious and worsening separatist insurgency in its southwestern Baluchistan province,[134] as well as rampant politically motivated violence in the megacity and business capital of Karachi.[135]

---

[129] "DOD New Briefing With British Army Lt. Gen. Adrian Bradshaw Via Teleconference From Afghanistan," Pentagon transcript, May 9, 2012; "Briefing by General John Allen, General Doug Lute, and Deputy National Security Advisor Ben Rhodes," Pentagon transcript, May 20, 2012.

[130] "Pakistan Hints It Will Soon Reopen NATO Supply Routes," McClatchy News, May 15, 2012.

[131] Quoted in "Pakistan Hints It Will Soon Reopen NATO Supply Routes," McClatchy News, May 15, 2012.

[132] "Pakistan Agrees to Reopen Supply Route," McClatchy News, May 16, 2012; "Pakistan Asks $5,000 For Each NATO Truck," *Washington Post*, May 17, 2012.

[133] "Levin and McCain: Don't Pay Pakistan Exorbitant Trucking Fees," *Foreign Policy* Cable (online), May 22, 2012.

[134] Baluchistan is in the throes of its fourth full-blown separatist rebellion since 1948. This current round of simmering (continued...)

The U.S. National Counterterrorism Center (NCTC) reports significant declines in terrorist incidents and related deaths in Pakistan since 2009. Nevertheless, its figures place the country third in the world on both measures, after Afghanistan and Iraq. Suicide bombing is a relatively new scourge in Pakistan. Only two such bombings were recorded there in 2002; that number rose to 84 in 2009, before dropping to 51 in 2010 and 41 in 2010. Still, Pakistan accounted for nearly half of all suicide bombing deaths worldwide in those years.[136] In recent years, militants have made sometimes spectacular attacks targeting the country's own military and intelligence institutions.[137] A nearly 20% drop in rates of Islamist attacks in 2011 as compared to the previous year generally was attributed to a combination of Pakistani military operations and U.S. drone strikes in the FATA, along with some improvement in law enforcement in major cities such as Islamabad and Lahore.[138] Still, some observers view the Islamabad government as sometimes being cowed by terrorists.[139]

The myriad and sometimes disparate Islamist militant groups operating in Pakistan, many of which have displayed mutual animosity in the past, became more intermingled and mutually supportive after 2009 (see text box below). U.S. leaders remain concerned that Al Qaeda terrorists operate with impunity on Pakistani territory, although the group apparently was weakened in recent years through the loss of key leaders and experienced operatives. The Tehrik-i-Taliban Pakistan (TTP) emerged as a coherent grouping in late 2007. This "Pakistani Taliban" is said to have representatives from each of Pakistan's seven tribal agencies, as well as from many of the "settled" districts abutting the FATA. The Quetta Shura Taliban of Mullah Omar is believed in that city, as well as Karachi. The Haqqani Network of Afghan insurgents is based in the North Waziristan and Kurram agencies of the FATA.

(...continued)

insurgency began in 2004 and is marked by serious human rights abuses on both sides. A new spike of violence caused more than 600 deaths in 2011. Over the decades of Pakistani independence, many of the ethnic Baluch who inhabit this relatively poor and underdeveloped province have engaged in armed conflict with federal government forces, variously seeking more equitable returns on the region's rich natural resources, greater autonomy under the country's federal system, or even outright independence and formation of a Baluch state. A largely incoherent insurgency is to date unable (and perhaps unwilling) to take on the Pakistani army directly, preferring instead sabotage missions against infrastructure targets. Faction leaders live in exile in several countries and have refrained from forming a united front, in part because of the province's strong tribal identities ("Baluchistan Separatists in Pakistan Beset by Divisions," McClatchy News, March 29, 2012).

[135] Already alarming levels of political and ethnic violence in Karachi began to spike in July 2011, when four days of mayhem left up to 95 people dead and prompted the Sindh government to issue "shoot on sight" orders to security forces. Another spasm of violence in August brought the 2011 death toll to more than 1,000 and elicited calls for army intervention. Targeted killings resumed in January 2012, and at least 800 people have been killed in politically-motivated attacks so far in 2012. The interplay of the city's ethnic-based political parties and heavily armed organized crime networks has only worsened with a large Pashtun migration into Karachi from western Pakistan ("Violence Escalates in Pakistan's Karachi," *Jane's Intelligence Weekly*, May 18, 2012).

[136] See the National Counterterrorism Center database at http://www.nctc.gov/wits/witsnextgen.html.

[137] In February 2011, a suicide bomber killed at least 27 soldiers at a military training center outside Peshawar; in March, a car bomb exploded near an ISI office in Faisalabad, Punjab, leaving some 32 people dead; in May, two suicide bombers killed at least 80 paramilitary cadets in the northwestern town of Charsadda. Later that month, militants raided Karachi's Mehran Naval Station, killing 10 and destroying two U.S.-supplied aircraft.

[138] "Pakistan: Militant Violence Down, But Fear Remains," Associated Press, December 7, 2011.

[139] Interior Minister Rehman Malik went so far as to thank Taliban militants for not undertaking anti-Shia attacks during the late 2011 Shiite ritual of Ashoura ("Pakistani Minister Thanks Taliban for Not Bombing," Associated Press, December 6, 2011).

Text Box: Islamist Militant Groups in Pakistan

Islamist militant groups operating in and from Pakistani territory are of five broad types:

- *Globally oriented* militants, especially Al Qaeda and its primarily Uzbek affiliates, operating out of the FATA and in the megacity of Karachi;

- *Afghanistan-oriented* militants, including the "Quetta shura" of Afghan Taliban leader Mullah Umar, believed to operate from the Baluchistan provincial capital of Quetta, as well as Karachi; the organization run by Jalaluddin Haqqani and his son Sirajuddin, in the North Waziristan and Kurram tribal agencies; and the Hizb-I Islami party led by Gulbuddin Hekmatyar (HiG), operating further north from the Bajaur tribal agency and Dir district;

- *India- and Kashmir-oriented* militants, especially the Lashkar-e-Taiba (LeT), Jaish-e-Mohammed (JeM), and Harakat ul-Mujahadeen (HuM), based in both the Punjab province and in Pakistan-held Kashmir;

- *Sectarian* militants, in particular the anti-Shia Sipah-e-Sahaba Pakistan (SSP) and its offshoot, Lashkar-e-Jhangvi (LeJ), the latter closely associated with Al Qaeda, operating mainly in Punjab; and

- *Domestically oriented*, largely Pashtun militants that in 2007 unified under the leadership of now-deceased Baitullah Mehsud as the Tehrik-i-Taliban Pakistan (TTP), then based in the South Waziristan tribal agency, with representatives from each of Pakistan's seven FATA agencies, later to incorporate the Tehreek-e-Nafaz-e-Shariat-e-Mohammadi (TNSM) led by Maulana Sufi Mohammed in the northwestern Malakand and Swat districts of the Khyber Pakhtunkhwa province.

Pakistan's densely populated Punjab province is home to numerous Islamist militant groups with regional and global jihadist aspirations. Notable among these is the Lashkar-e-Taiba (LeT), a U.S.-designated terrorist group with long-standing ties to the ISI. The U.S. government sees the LeT posing a growing threat to U.S. national security. The Raymond Davis affair may have exposed new and independent U.S. intelligence operations against the LeT in Pakistan.[140] Many analysts now identify the LeT as the most dangerous terrorist group operating in South Asia, one that could grow into a global threat if left unchecked.[141] LeT's ostensible charity wing, Jamaat-ud-Dawa (JuD, also proscribed under U.S. and international law) has an expanding and diversified infrastructure inside Pakistan.[142]

Husain Haqqani, Pakistan's Ambassador to the United States from 2008 to 2011, decries his country's apparent fixation on U.S. violations of its sovereignty while paying little or no heed to combating the "jihadist ideology" that has cost tens of thousands of Pakistani lives in recent years. He recently has upbraided the country's Supreme Court for directing its energy toward dislodging the civilian government rather than seeking to bring terrorist leaders to justice. In Haqqani's view, the misguided national mindset was encouraged by military dictators as a means of redirecting public attention: "Anti-Western Sentiment and a sense of collective victimhood were cultivated as a substitute for serious debate on social and economic policy."[143]

---

[140] "A Shooting in Pakistan Reveals Fraying Alliance," *New York Times*, March 13, 2011.

[141] See, for example, Ashley Tellis, "The Menace That Is Lashkar-e-Taiba," Carnegie Endowment for International Peace Policy Outlook, March 2012.

[142] By one account, JuD operates more than 300 offices, mosques, and madrassas, 200 health centers and 7 hospitals, along with hundreds of commercial ventures, and one of the country's largest ambulance fleets (Muhammad Amir Rana, "The Case of JuD" (op-ed), *Dawn* (Karachi), March 25, 2012).

[143] Husain Haqqani, "How Pakistan Let Terrorism Fester" (op-ed), *New York Times*, May 11, 2012.

Domestic Military Operations

The Pakistan army has deployed at least 150,000 regular and paramilitary troops in western Pakistan in response to the surge in militancy there, and the army has seen more than 3,000 of its soldiers killed in combat. All seven FATA agencies and adjacent regions have been affected by conflict; 2009 offensives in the Swat Valley and South Waziristan were notable. As noted above, U.S. government assessments paint a discouraging picture of recent efforts. In most areas where Pakistani military offensives have taken place, the "clearing" phase of operations has met with some successes, but the "holding" phase has proven more difficult, and "building" is considered impossible to initiate so long as the civilian administration's capacity is severely limited.[144] Independent analyses reach similar conclusions, saying Pakistani military offensives in Swat and FATA from 2009 to 2011 had mixed results, at best. The army has seen major successes in at least temporarily dislodging militants but, outside of Swat, military gains have not led to sustained counterinsurgency progress, and no notable militant leaders have been killed or captured in ground operations.[145]

The Pakistani air force claims to have flown more than 5,500 combat sorties over the FATA, dropping more than 10,000 bombs—80% of them laser-guided—and destroying 4,600 targets.[146] Sometimes bloody fighting has continued in the FATA as government forces press sporadic offensives in the Kurram and Khyber agencies, in particular. Spring 2012 battles in Khyber—home to the TTP-allied Lashkar-i-Islam (LI) led by Mangal Bagh—reportedly have driven more than 500,000 civilians from their homes. After years of trying, the Pakistani army appears to be having meaningful successes in degrading LI's capabilities.[147] Yet a simmering insurgency still affects most FATA agencies. In January, TTP militants overran a Frontier Constabulary fort in South Waziristan and executed 15 soldiers. Moreover, Bajaur suffered its worst militant attack in more than a year when a TTP suicide bomber killed dozens of people in May 2012, the local Bajaur Levies commander and his deputy among them, in apparent retaliation for the killing of an Al Qaeda operative killed by those security forces in 2011.[148]

Yet, by many accounts the North Waziristan agency—home to the Al Qaeda- and Taliban-allied Haqqani Network and the TTP forces of Hafiz Gul Bahadar, among others—is currently the most important haven for both Afghan- and Pakistan-oriented militants. Pakistani officials have continued to demur on urgent U.S. requests that their military move into what many consider the "final" militant haven of North Waziristan, saying they need to consolidate the areas newly under their control.[149] Moreover, Pakistan's military forces are new to counterinsurgency and

---

[144] See the White House Report on Afghanistan and Pakistan, September 2011.

[145] See, for example, Daud Khattak, "Evaluating Pakistan's Offensives in Swat and FATA," *CTC Sentinel*, October 2011.

[146] Pakistan's Air Chief Marshall cited in "PAF Made 5,500 Strike Sorties Over FATA," *News* (Karachi), November 15, 2011.

[147] "Pakistan Fighting Uproots Hundreds of Thousands," Agence France Presse, May 14, 2012; Daud Khattak, "Mangal Bagh and LI Marginalized in Khyber Agency," Combating Terrorism Center at West Point (online), April 23, 2012.

[148] "Suicide Bomber Attacks Checkpoint in Pakistan," *New York Times*, May 4, 2012.

[149] When pressed by Senate Armed Services Committee members to explain why Pakistan was not going after the Haqqani Network and Quetta Shura, Centcom Commander General Mattis offered three key reasons: (1) "their difficult relationship with India" that compels them to maintain a hedge; (2) the difficult terrain of the FATA; and (3) the impact of mid-2010 flooding, which diverted Pakistani military resources away from counterinsurgency efforts ("Senate Armed Services Committee Holds Hearing on the Fiscal 2012 Defense Authorization Request for the Special Operations Command and the U.S. Central Command," CQ Transcriptions, March 1, 2011).

---

demonstrate only limited capacity to undertake effective nonconventional warfare. Pakistani leaders have complained that the United States has been slow in providing the kind of hardware needed for this effort, but Islamabad's July 2011 ejection of U.S. military trainers has dramatically hindered U.S. efforts to bolster Pakistan's COIN capabilities.

FATA Militancy Dynamics and Possible Negotiations

Independent analysts assert that Pakistan's military operations and "divide-and-conquer" political approach, combined with drone strikes and internal militant power struggles, effectively splintered the Pakistani Taliban in 2011, leaving scores of smaller and weaker factions, most of which do not take orders from nominal TTP leader Hakimullah Mehsud. This development may explain the major decrease in suicide bomb attacks in Pakistan last year.[150] The apparently volatile Mehsud has longstanding feuds with militant commanders Maulvi Nazir of South Waziristan and Hafiz Gul Bahadar of North Waziristan, both of whom have struck truce deals with the government.[151] More recently, he is said to have been ordered killed by his own former deputy, Wali-ur-Rehman, another senior South Waziristan militant commander who reportedly feels Mehsud has made the TTP too close to Al Qaeda Arabs.[152]

Within this setting, Pakistani civilian officials suggested in late 2011 that they were open to new negotiations with TTP militants, especially as the United States began to favor talks with the Afghan Taliban. Deputy TTP chief Maulvi Faqir Muhammad claimed that meetings with government representatives began in November. Rawalpindi remained silent on the alleged initiative, however, and domestic and international concerns arose given the failure of similar efforts in the FATA in 2005, 2006, and 2008 that appeared to leave the militants in a stronger position. Weeks later, a TTP spokesman denied that any negotiations were underway and, in March, Faqir reportedly was removed from his TTP position, likely for engaging in dialogue with the government, a demotion that enraged his lieutenants in the Bajaur agency.[153]

Yet negotiations do appear to have taken place and may be continuing. By some accounts, Afghan Taliban leader Mullah Omar has pressured Pakistani militants to make peace with the Pakistani army as a means of reinforcing his own ranks. Al Qaeda and Haqqani group interlocutors are said to have mediated an intra-militant pact to unify four major militant factions under Omar's leadership and based in the two Waziristan agencies. This "Shura-i-Muraqba"—comprised of the Haqqanis and commanders Wali-ur-Rehman, Maulvi Nazir, and Gul Bahadar—is to direct its hostility solely toward Afghanistan, unlike the TTP, which is at war with the Pakistani state.[154] The Haqqanis are widely believed to be seeking to forward their own cause by ending the anti-

[150] "Pak Taliban No Longer a Unified Group," *News* (Karachi), November 15, 2011; "Pakistani Taliban Splintering Into Factions," Associated Press, December 4, 2011.

[151] In mid- 2011, Nazir, who has been honoring a 2007 peace deal with the Pakistani government, vowed to escalate attacks on American forces in Afghanistan in retaliation for intensified drone strikes on his region. Nazir is believed to have more than 1,000 fighters at his disposal ("Pakistan Militant Group Vows to Escalate Fight in Afghanistan," Reuters, June 8, 2011).

[152] "Pakistan Taliban Commanders 'At Each Other's Throats,'" Reuters, January 3, 2012.

[153] "As Pakistan Eyes Peace Talks With the Taliban, Anxiety Builds," *Los Angeles Times*, November 13, 2011; "Taliban, Pakistan Said to Have Started Peace Talks," Reuters, November 21, 2011; "Leadership Rift Emerges in Pakistani Taliban," *New York Times*, March 6, 2012.

[154] "'Mullah Omar is Pushing TTP to Reconcile With Govt,'" *Express Tribune* (Karachi), November 26, 2011; "In War on NATO, Militants Call for Truce With Pakistan," McClatchy News, January 3, 2012; "Militant Groups in Pakistan Form United Front," *Washington Post*, January 3, 2012.

Pakistan insurgency and so focusing FATA militants' attention on Afghanistan, a shift that no doubt would be welcomed by the Pakistani military.[155]

New Counterterrorism Pressure on Islamabad

Pakistan's status as a site and source of terrorist international activity continues to be a central concern of the U.S. and other world governments. In April 2012, the U.S. government offered a $10 million reward for information leading to the conviction of Pakistani citizen Hafiz Saeed, leader of the terrorist group that undertook the 2008 Mumbai attack. The news was welcomed by India, but caused further animosity in U.S.-Pakistan relations. Prime Minister Gilani criticized the move as a "negative message" that would "further widen the trust deficit" between the two countries. Opposition lawmakers used even stronger language in their denunciation of the "ridiculous" U.S. announcement.[156]

Also in April, scores of well-armed militants assaulted a prison in the northwestern town of Bannu near the FATA and freed nearly 400 prisoners, including one terrorist sentenced to death for a 2003 plot to kill then-President-General Pervez Musharraf. A subsequent government inquiry concluded that local police, paramilitary forces, civil administrators, and the intelligence agencies were "collectively responsible" for the lapse.[157] The raid successfully bolstered Pakistani Taliban force levels and was a major propaganda coup that fueled already acute concerns about the effectiveness of the Pakistani state's security apparatus.

During a May 2012 visit to New Delhi, India, Secretary of State Clinton made a point of once again requesting that Pakistan "do more" to clear its territory of terrorist sanctuaries, and she chastised the Islamabad government for taking insufficient action against Hafiz Saeed.[158] U.S. officials remain acutely concerned about the apparent impunity with which Pakistan-based extremist and militant groups are able to act. The senior Afghan Taliban leadership believed to be in Quetta and Karachi, the Haqqani Network based in the North Waziristan and Kurram tribal agencies, and U.S.-designated Foreign Terrorist Organizations such as LeT, Jaish-e-Mohammed, and others in Pakistan's Punjabi heartland appear to remain significant threats to the United States and its allies, including those in Islamabad's civilian government.[159]

Pakistan, Terrorism, and U.S. Nationals[160]

Long-standing worries that American citizens were being recruited and employed in Islamist terrorism by Pakistan-based elements became more acute in 2010. In May of that year, Faisal Shahzad, a naturalized U.S. citizen of Pakistani origin, attempted to detonate a large, but crudely

---

[155] See the comments of Daniel Markey in "Gauging Taliban Moves in Pakistan" (interview), Council on Foreign Relations, March 8, 2012.

[156] Quoted in "Pakistan Lawmakers Criticize U.S. Reward for Militant Leader," *New York Times*, April 6, 2012.

[157] "Bannu Jailbreak: Police, Civil Admin, and Spy Agencies Held Responsible," *Daily Times* (Lahore), May 17, 2012.

[158] "Pakistan Dragging Its Feet on Mumbai Mastermind: Clinton," Reuters, May 7, 2012.

[159] Earlier in 2012, the U.S. Ambassador to Afghanistan reportedly sent a top-secret cable to Washington warning that the persistence of Afghan insurgent havens in Pakistan was putting the entire U.S. strategy in Afghanistan at risk ("Cable: Pakistan Havens a Threat," *Washington Post*, February 25, 2012).

[160] See also CRS Report R41416, *American Jihadist Terrorism: Combating a Complex Threat*, by Jerome P. Bjelopera.

---

constructed car bomb in New York City's Times Square. The Pakistani Taliban claimed responsibility for the attempted bombing, and the culprit himself confessed to having received bomb-making training in western Pakistan. Four months later, Shahzad received a mandatory life sentence in prison. Other cases linking U.S. citizens and residents with Islamist extremism in Pakistan and terrorist plots against American targets are abundant.[161]

At least one Pakistani-born American was complicit in the 2008 terrorist attack on Mumbai, India. In 2009, federal prosecutors charged David Coleman Headley, a Chicagoan convert to Islam, with traveling to Mumbai five times from 2006 to 2008 as scout for the attack by the Pakistan-based LeT terrorist group; he subsequently pleaded guilty to the charges. His case was perhaps the first in which a former Pakistani military officer was directly linked to terrorism suspects in the United States. Headley and another Pakistan-born Chicagoan, Tahawwur Rana (a Canadian national), are believed to have reported to a retired Pakistani major suspected of being an LeT contact. Headley also interacted with Ilayas Kashmiri, a now-deceased former Pakistani special forces commando with close ties to Al Qaeda. The Indian government energetically petitioned Washington for direct access to Headley as part of its own investigative efforts. Access was granted with an extensive interrogation in 2010; Indian officials later said the information gleaned established an official Pakistani role in the Mumbai attack.

In May 2011, a Chicago court heard testimony in Rana's trial (Rana was charged with material support of terrorism related to the Mumbai attack). Three senior LeT members were also indicted in the case—LeT chief Hafez Saeed among them—along with a purported ISI officer identified as "Major Iqbal." Headley, the prosecution's star witness, detailed links between the ISI and terrorism, and so added to already fraught U.S.-Pakistan relations and suspicions about official Pakistani involvement in supporting Islamist militancy. Rana subsequently was acquitted on charges related to the Mumbai attack, but was found guilty of aiding the LeT and of conspiring to attack a Danish newspaper.

---

[161] In late 2009, Pakistani authorities arrested five young Americans reported missing from their homes in Virginia. The Muslim men are believed to have had extensive coded email contacts with Pakistan-based terrorist groups. A Pakistani court charged them with financing and plotting terrorist attacks and, in June 2010, the so-called Virginia Five were sentenced to 10 years of labor in prison for conspiring against the Pakistani state and helping to finance a militant organization. Also, the case of would-be terrorist bomber Najibullah Zazi—an Afghan national and legal U.S. resident arrested in 2009 after months of FBI surveillance—seemed to demonstrate that terrorist training camps continue to operate in the FATA, where Zazi is said to have learned bomb-making skills at an Al Qaeda-run compound. In July 2010, the Justice Department unsealed new terrorism-related charges against Zazi and four other men, including a Pakistani-American, who allegedly had plans to bomb the New York subways. Other Americans have received terrorist training in Pakistan, including Bryant Neal Vinas, who confessed to plotting a bomb attack against the Long Island Railroad in New York.

In April 2011, a Pakistani-American Virginia man was sentenced to 23 years in prison for plotting a series of bomb attacks on the Washington Metro system. In May, three Pakistani-American Floridians were among six people indicted on federal charges of providing material support to and encouraging violence by the Pakistani Taliban. In August, a Maryland teenager from Pakistan was reported to be in U.S. custody after he allegedly agreed to help Pennsylvania's "Jihad Jane" raise money and recruits for the jihadist cause. In December, a Virginia resident from Pakistan pled guilty to charges of producing a jihadist recruiting video on behalf of the LeT; he was later sentenced to 12 years in prison. In February 2012, a Pakistani national and legal Maryland resident confessed to joining Al Qaeda and plotting to blow up gasoline tanks in the United States, as well as assassinate the Pakistani president.

Progress in Pakistan-India Relations

Background and Resumption of the Composite Dialogue

Three full-scale wars—in 1947-1948, 1965, and 1971—and a constant state of military preparedness on both sides of their mutual border have marked more than six decades of bitter rivalry between Pakistan and India. The acrimonious partition of British India into two successor states in 1947 and the unresolved issue of Kashmiri sovereignty have been major sources of tension between these two nuclear-armed countries. Both have built large defense establishments at significant cost to economic and social development. A bilateral "Composite Dialogue" was reengaged in 2004 and realized some modest, but still meaningful successes, including a formal cease-fire along the entire shared frontier, and unprecedented trade and people-to-people contacts across the Kashmiri Line of Control (LOC). The dialogue is meant to bring about "peaceful settlement of all bilateral issues, including Jammu and Kashmir, to the satisfaction of both sides."[162] Yet 2008 saw significant deterioration in Pakistan-India relations, especially following the large-scale November terrorist attack on Mumbai, India, that killed some 165 civilians (including 6 Americans) and left the peace process largely moribund. More broadly, militarized territorial disputes over Kashmir, the Siachen Glacier, and the Sir Creek remain unresolved. In 2010, conflict over water resources emerged as another exacerbating factor in the bilateral relationship.

Pakistani leaders, like many independent observers, believe that regional peace is inextricably linked to a solution of the Kashmir dispute. Under the Obama Administration, the U.S. government has continued its long-standing policy of keeping distance from that dispute and refraining from any mediation role. By some accounts, Pakistan and India are also fighting a "shadow war" inside Afghanistan with spies and proxies, with all high-visibility attacks comng against Indian targets. Islamabad accuses New Delhi of using Indian consulates in Afghanistan as bases for malevolent interference in Pakistan's western regions, even as there is scant available evidence to support such claims.

Following the 2008 Mumbai attack, the New Delhi government focused on holding Islamabad accountable for the existence of anti-India terrorists groups in Pakistan, some of them suspected of receiving direct support from official Pakistani elements, and India essentially refused to reengage the full spectrum of Composite Dialogue issues. Yet, with an early 2011 meeting of foreign secretaries, India agreed to resume peace talks without overt mention of the centrality of the terrorism issue. Days later, the two governments announced that high-level peace talks would be resumed after a hiatus of more than two years.

Following the brief "cricket diplomacy" of March 2011—Prime Minister Gilani had accepted his Indian counterpart's invitation to watch a match in India—bilateral talks between home secretaries produced an agreement to establish a "terror hotline" between the respective ministries. Under the resumed dialogue process, the two countries' commerce secretaries met in April 2011 for talks on greater economic and commercial cooperation. A June meeting of foreign secretaries in Islamabad appeared unexpectedly positive to many, with the two officials agreeing to expand confidence-building measures related to both nuclear and conventional weapons, as

---

[162] See the January 6, 2004, Joint Statement at http://www.indianembassy.org/press_release/2004/jan/07 htm.

well as to increase trade and travel across the Kashmiri LOC.[163] A July Joint Statement produced with Foreign Minister Khar's New Delhi visit was widely taken as a successful representation of a peace process back on track after a more than two-year hiatus.[164] The two countries' trade ministers met in New Delhi in September and agreed to take steps to further liberalize their relatively paltry bilateral trade (the necessity of moving exports through Dubai raises transaction costs, slows deliveries, and inflates prices). India also dropped its long-standing opposition to a proposed EU initiative that would waive duties on Pakistani exports from its flood-ravaged areas.

The circumstances of OBL's death were relevant to the course of relations between Pakistan and India. Indian Prime Minister Manmohan Singh called the killing "a significant step forward" and expressed hope that it would represent a decisive blow to AQ and other terrorist groups. At the same time, however, New Delhi is concerned that the development is hastening a U.S. withdrawal from Afghanistan in ways that could be harmful to India's foreign policy interests. New Delhi also saw the discovery of OBL in Pakistan as an opportunity to more energetically press its demands that Islamabad extradite the alleged perpetrators of the 2008 Mumbai terrorist attack, Lashkar-e-Taiba figures believed to be in Pakistan, as well as other most-wanted anti-India terrorists such as organized crime figure Dawood Ibrahim.[165]

When Afghan President Karzai made a long-planned trip to New Delhi in October 2011 and inked a new "strategic framework" with India—Kabul's first such 21st century agreement with any country—Pakistan's fears of strategic encirclement became more acute, especially in light of Afghanistan's acceptance of future Indian assistance in training and equipping its security forces. Kabul's floundering efforts to find rapprochement with the Taliban may be behind Karzai's decision to link Afghanistan more closely to India. Although the Afghan President took pains to insist that the pact was not directed at any country, some analysts saw it as a highly provocative development that could make it more difficult to wean Pakistan away from its apparent reliance on militant proxies in Afghanistan.[166]

Positive Recent Developments

The current tenor of Pakistan's relations with India is better than it has been in many years. The Pakistan-supported separatist rebellion in Indian-held Kashmir is at its lowest ebb since it began in 1989, and the region has been mostly quiet since mid-2010. In late 2011, Pakistan's government vowed to grant normal, Most-Favored Nation (MFN) trade status to India by the end of 2012. A U.S. State Department spokeswoman called the news a "very, very big deal" that could bring new prosperity to the region. Lower tariffs and fewer visa restrictions could boost the value of bilateral trade as much as tenfold from the $2.5 billion seen in 2010, as well as build "peace constituencies" in both countries. Perhaps most importantly, Islamabad's offer to move toward freer bilateral trade—manifest recently by its conversion from a "positive list" of items permitted for import from India to a "negative list" of only those items prohibited—suggests that Pakistan's long-held insistence on progress with the "core issue" of Kashmir as a prerequisite for movement

---

[163] See the June 24, 2011, Joint Statement at http://www.mofa.gov.pk/Press_Releases/2011/June/Pr_218.htm.

[164] See the July 27, 2011, text at http://meaindia nic.in/mystart.php?id=530517878.

[165] In May 2012, the U.S. Treasury Department tagged two of Ibrahim's lieutenants as Specially Designated Narcotics Traffickers. Ibrahim himself received such designation in 2006 and has been a Specially Designated Global Terrorist since 2003 (see http://www.treasury.gov/press-center/press-releases/Pages/tg1579.aspx).

[166] "Karzai Picks Partnership With India Over Pakistan," *Financial Times* (London), October 5, 2011; "Indo-Afghan Pact Threatens Relations With Pakistan," *Jane's Intelligence Weekly*, October 5, 2011.

in other areas may be receding. Moreover, there have been no terrorist attacks in India traced to Pakistan in more than three years, a significant gap given the pace of previous attacks.

In April 2012, President Zardari made a brief and unofficial visit to India that included a lunch meeting with Prime Minister Singh. It was the first such travel by a Pakistani head of state since 2005. Only days later an avalanche at the remote Siachen Glacier in the Himalayas killed 139 Pakistani soldiers based in the area. For nearly 30 years Pakistani and Indian troops have faced off in this harsh environment that is part of the former princely state of Kashmir. The avalanche tragedy brought renewed attention to the apparent senselessness of conflict over a region with negligible military value, but both governments remain intransigent and deny any plans to redeploy their forces.

In May 2012, after nearly two decades of negotiations, Pakistan and India signed pacts with Turkmenistan to build a pipeline through Afghanistan that would carry up to 90 million cubic meters of natural gas each day. The 1,100-mile-long pipeline, projected to cost at least $7.6 billion to build, is enthusiastically supported by Washington as a perfect example of the kind of regional energy integration envisioned in the New Silk Road Initiative, as well as an effective bypassing of Iran, a country the United States seeks to isolate.[167] However, many independent observers are deeply skeptical that security circumstances inside Afghanistan will improve enough in the foreseeable future to win investor confidence.

Despite circumstances that provide many analysts with cause for cautious optimism, so long as Islamist militancy emanates from Pakistan and threatens India, New Delhi's willingness to make meaningful concessions will most likely be seriously constrained. India remains unsatisfied with Pakistan's refusal/inability to bring the Mumbai terrorism masterminds to justice, and the continued freedom in Pakistan of LeT chief Hafiz Saeed is a major sticking point. Islamabad continues to bear criticism from New Delhi for not acting on alleged "concrete evidence" sufficient to prosecute Saeed and other suspected Mumbai attack culprits.[168] India also seeks extradition of Ibrahim and several Indian Mujahedeen leaders believed to be residing in Pakistan.[169] Yet movement on the economic front could reinforce already significant motives for both governments to eschew open conflict. As ever, the calculations made by Pakistan's generals are considered key to determining the future course of relations.

Pakistan-China Relations

Pakistan and China have enjoyed a generally close and mutually beneficial relationship over several decades. Pakistan served as a link between Beijing and Washington in 1971, as well as a bridge to the Muslim world for China during the 1980s. China's continuing role as a primary arms supplier for Pakistan began in the 1960s and included helping to build a number of arms

---

[167] See the relevant statements of State Department spokeswoman Victoria Nuland, Daily Briefing transcript, May 23, 2012.

[168] A leading American expert on the LeT contends that Pakistani officials are actively pressuring the group to refrain from launching further major terrorist attacks in India, and he suggests that, because the organization enjoys considerable popular support in Pakistan, efforts to dismantle it should be gradual in order to avoid serious backlash (statement of Stephen Tankel, "House Homeland Security Subcommittee Holds Hearing on U.S. Homeland Security Threats From Pakistan," QC Transcripts, May 3, 2011).

[169] "India Presses Pak to Use Fresh Info to Nail 11/26 Accused," Press Trust of India, May 24, 2012.

factories in Pakistan, as well as supplying complete weapons systems. Chinese companies and workers are now pervasive in the Pakistani economy. Beijing intends to build two new civilian nuclear reactors in Pakistan in what would be an apparent violation of international guidelines. During Chinese Premier Wen Jiabao's late 2010 visit to Islamabad, the governments signed 12 Memoranda of Understanding covering a broad range of cooperative efforts and designated 2011 as the "Year of China-Pakistan Friendship." Pakistani and Chinese businesses also signed contracts worth some $15 billion covering cooperation in oil and gas, mining, space technology, heavy machinery, manufacturing, and other areas. This added to the nearly $20 billion worth of government-to-government agreements reached.[170]

Pakistan appeared to react quickly and with purpose in August 2011 when Beijing publically blamed Islamist militants trained in Pakistan for terrorist activities in China's western Xinjiang province. ISI Director Pasha was dispatched to Beijing with the apparent aim of assuaging China. In 2012, Beijing has become more open in expressing concerns that Uighur separatists train and find haven in Pakistan; Chinese allegations that Uighur militants have close links with other Pakistan-based terrorist groups put stresses on bilateral relations.[171]

As U.S.-India ties deepen and U.S.-Pakistan ties have deteriorated, many observers see Islamabad becoming ever more reliant on its friendship with Beijing. Pakistani leaders became notably more and perhaps overly effusive in their expressions of closeness with China in 2011.[172] Prime Minister Gilani's May 2011 visit there—coming shortly after the Abbottabad raid—elicited no major new embrace from Beijing, but the Chinese government did insist that the West "must respect" Pakistan's sovereignty, and it agreed to expedite delivery to Pakistan of 50 JF-17 fighter jets equipped with upgraded avionics (Islamabad is also negotiating with Beijing for the purchase of six new submarines for as much as $3 billion in what would be the largest-ever bilateral defense purchase).

The United States and China share an interest in seeing Pakistan's counterterrorism capabilities strengthened. While Beijing continues to view its relationship with Pakistan as providing a means of balancing against and perhaps even containing India's regional aspirations, it recognizes that Pakistan-based terrorist groups could trigger the kind of full-blown Pakistan-India crisis that would do great harm to Chinese economic interests in the region. These dynamics provide a basis for greater U.S.-China coordination "to improve the discipline and capacity of Pakistan's military and intelligence services," and perhaps even elicit Chinese pressure on Islamabad to dismantle global jihadist groups such as LeT. Moreover—and despite diverging interests on India's regional role—the United States and China could expand cooperation into other vital areas, including nonproliferation, governance, and economic growth in Pakistan.[173]

---

[170] December 19, 2010, Joint Statement at http://www.mofa.gov.pk/Press_Releases/2010/Dec/Pr_310.htm.

[171] "China Points Finger at Pakistan Again," *Wall Street Journal*, March 8, 2012; "China Says Wanted Militants Use Nearby Countries to Stage Attacks," *New York Times*, April 6, 2012.

[172] For example, in Beijing in May, Prime Minister Gilani spoke of "the reality of this abiding friendship between our peoples, which is manifested in abundant goodwill, spontaneous affinity, inestimable love and affection, an enduring romance that transcends all other considerations" ("Remarks of the Prime Minister at the Reception to Commemorate the 60th Anniversary of the Establishment of Diplomatic Relations Between Pakistan and China," Foreign Ministry transcript, May 20, 2011).

[173] Daniel Markey, "Pakistan Contingencies," in Paul Stares, et al., *Managing Instability on China's Periphery*, Council on Foreign Relations Center for Preventive Action, September 2011.

Chinese military and diplomatic support for Pakistan continues to hinder India's regional ambitions. Indeed, as the United States seeks to deepen its partnership with India, China's geostrategic reliance on Pakistan is likely to grow. Yet China's own aspirations and interests seem to dictate that Beijing not make its Pakistan policies with a narrow focus on balancing India alone. A wider set of interests suggests that the "all-weather friendship" with Pakistan no longer entails the kind of blanket support Islamabad had come to expect in the past.[174] The Chinese government reportedly is unlikely to place itself in the middle of any U.S.-Pakistani rift, nor has it shown any desire to replace Washington as Islamabad's primary foreign benefactor.[175]

Pakistan-Iran Relations and U.S. Sanctions

Pakistan's relations with its Shia Muslim-majority neighbor Iran have long been troubled by differences over Afghanistan (the two countries actively supported opposing sides in the Afghan civil war of the 1990s) and by the presence in Pakistan of anti-Shia terrorist groups.[176] Yet the two countries have cooperated in some areas and both governments aspire to realize the long-anticipated completion of a pipeline that would carry natural gas from Iran to feed Pakistan's unmet energy demands. Tehran claims that construction on its side of the border is complete and it reportedly has offered to provide Pakistan with $500 million to finance construction on its side after a Chinese consortium withdrew its involvement in the project.[177]

As the U.S. government seeks to further isolate Iran with sanctions related to its nuclear program, Washington has repeatedly expressed opposition to this pipeline project. In February, Secretary of State Clinton told a House panel that "actually beginning construction of such a pipeline [on the Pakistani side of the border] ... would violate our Iran sanctions law." The Administration has made its concerns "absolutely clear" to Islamabad, which remains insistent that it will complete the project.[178] Tehran's further efforts to skirt international sanctions have included seeking barter deals with Pakistan to trade oil for huge stocks of wheat and rice.

Nuclear Weapons Proliferation and Security[179]

The security of Pakistan's nuclear arsenal, materials, and technologies continues to be a top-tier U.S. concern, especially as Islamist militants have expanded their geographic influence there.

---

[174] Harsh Pant, "The Pakistan Thorn in China-India-U.S. Relations," *Washington Quarterly*, December 2011; Evan Feigenbaum, "China's Pakistan Conundrum," *Foreign Affairs* (online), December 4, 2011; Richard Weitz, "How Pakistan Kids Itself on China," *Diplomat* (Tokyo), December 28, 2011.

[175] "Pakistan Courts China as Relations With U.S. Grow Strained," *Washington Post*, June 22, 2011; Andrew Small, "How All-Weather Are the Ties?," *Pragati* (Chennai, online), August 5, 2011; "China Treads Carefully Amid US-Pakistan Rift," Reuters, October 4, 2011.

[176] Sectarian groups such as LeJ have murdered hundreds of Pakistani Shias with a great degree of impunity; the culprits are rarely caught or punished (Pakistan's Shias Fear Sectarian Attacks," BBC News, May 9, 2012).

[177] "Iran Offers 500m Dollars to Pakistan for Gas Pipeline Project," BBC Monitoring South Asia, April 26, 2012.

[178] "House Appropriations Subcommittee on State, Foreign Operations, and Related Programs Holds Hearing on the Proposed Fiscal 2013 Appropriations for the State Department and Foreign Operations," CQ Transcripts, February 29, 2012. Islamabad contends that the project "is beyond the scope of relevant UN resolutions" and it intends to see the project completed in 2014 (Foreign Affairs Ministry press briefing transcript, January 26, 2012).

[179] See also CRS Report RL34248, *Pakistan's Nuclear Weapons: Proliferation and Security Issues*, by Paul K. Kerr and Mary Beth Nikitin.

Pakistan has in the recent past been a source of serious illicit proliferation to aspiring weapons states. The illicit nuclear proliferation network allegedly overseen by Pakistani metallurgist A.Q. Khan was disrupted after its exposure in 2004, but neither Khan himself—a national hero in Pakistan—nor any of his alleged Pakistani co-conspirators have faced criminal charges in the case, and analysts warn that parts of the network may still be intact. While most analysts and U.S. officials believe Pakistan's nuclear security is much improved in recent years, there is ongoing concern that Pakistan's nuclear know-how or technologies remain prone to leakage.[180] Moreover, recent reports indicate that Pakistan is rapidly growing its nuclear weapons arsenal, perhaps in response to recent U.S. moves to engage civil nuclear cooperation with India, which the Obama Administration wants to see join major international nonproliferation regimes.[181] Pakistan's appears to be the world's most rapidly growing nuclear arsenal at a time that China is planning to build two new nuclear reactors there in apparent violation of Nuclear Suppliers Group guidelines. The proposed deal poses a dilemma for the Obama Administration, which has requested that Beijing justify the plan and seeks its approval through international fora.

Deteriorated Economic Circumstances

Overview and IMF Bailout

Persistent inflation and unemployment, along with serious food and energy shortages, elicit considerable economic anxiety in Pakistan and weigh heavily on the civilian government. All of these existing problems were hugely exacerbated by devastating flooding in the summer of 2010 (according to the Finance Ministry, Pakistan's economy suffered some $10 billion in losses related to this flooding) and again in September 2011. Corruption is another serious obstacle to Pakistan's economic development, harming both domestic and foreign investment rates, and public confidence, as well as creating skeptical international aid donors.[182] Foreign direct investment plummeted to under $2.2 billion in FY2010/2011, less than half of the $5.4 billion garnered two years earlier. Most analysts identify increasing militancy as the main cause for the decline, although global recession and political instability in Islamabad are also major factors. In the assessment of international financial institutions, Pakistan's economic priorities are addressing inflation, containing the budget deficit, reviving growth, and meeting the challenge posed by higher global oil prices. **Figure 3** and **Figure 4** show that for many years Pakistan's economic development levels were similar to India's; for much of the post-independence period, Pakistan's GDP per capita was slightly higher than India's. However, in the early 2000s, India's

---

[180] In July 2011, Joint Chiefs Chairman Admiral Mullen reiterated having a high level of confidence in the safety and security of Pakistan's nuclear arsenal, but such public assurances may not match privately expressed U.S. concerns ("Mullen: Pakistani Nuclear Controls Should Avert Any Insider Threat," Global Security Newswire," July 8, 2011; "Pakistan's Nuclear Security Troubles," *Jane's Islamic Affairs Analyst*, July 26, 2011).

[181] Pakistan is believed to be deploying upwards of 100 nuclear warheads and has significantly accelerated its production of uranium and plutonium. Analysts also suspect that Pakistan has begun construction of a fourth plutonium-producing reactor at its Khushab complex ("Pakistan's Nuclear Surge," *Newsweek*, May 15, 2011).

[182] For 2011, Berlin-based Transparency International placed Pakistan 134th out of 183 countries in its annual ranking of world corruption levels and 118th of 142 on its global competitiveness index. A major 2011 public opinion survey found that combating corruption was by far the most important priority identified by respondents, with fully 48% ranking corruption as the "greatest threat to Pakistan" (in second place was the United States, named as the greatest threat by 29%). Bribery, nepotism, and profit from public office were each identified as "huge problems" by about three-quarters of respondents (see http://www.transparency.org; Joel Faulkner Rogers, "Public Opinion in Pakistan and the Newfound Popularity of Pakistan Tehreek-e-Insaf (PTI)," YouGov-Cambridge, December 23, 2011).

growth shot upward while Pakistan's remained flat, and today India—with roughly seven times the population of Pakistan—enjoys higher national wealth figures even on a per capita basis.

Figure 3. Indian and Pakistani Gross National Product at PPP, 1980-2011

(in billions of U.S. dollars)

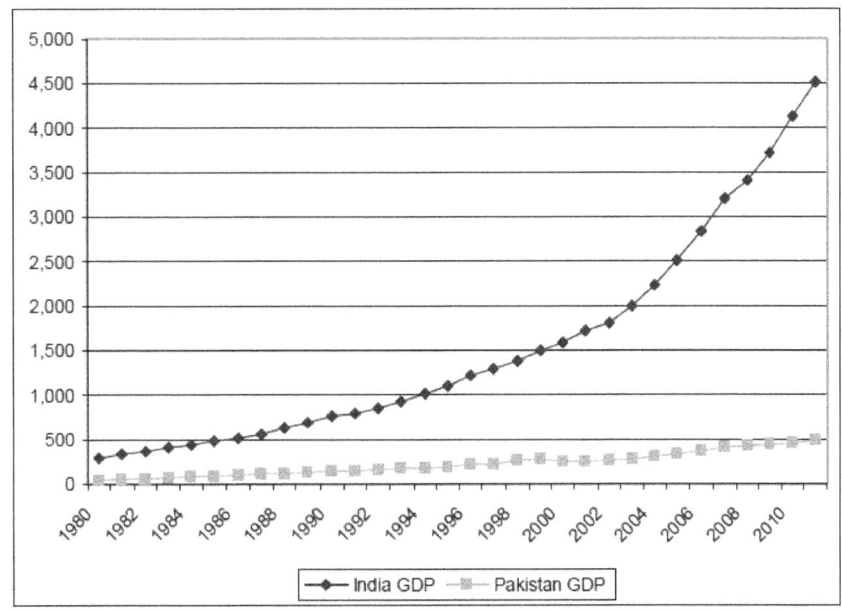

Source: Economist Intelligence Unit.

Figure 4. Indian and Pakistani Gross National Product per Capita, 1980-2011

(in U.S. dollars)

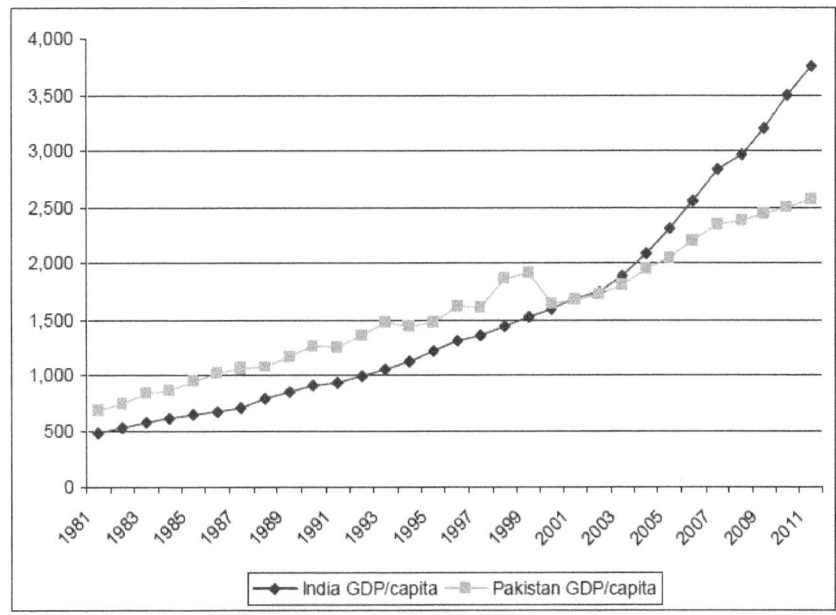

Source: Economist Intelligence Unit.

A 2008 balance-of-payments crisis led Islamabad to seek multi-billion dollar loans from the International Monetary Fund (IMF). The current IMF-supported program is a 34-month, $11.3 billion Stand-By Arrangement first approved in November 2008, augmented in 2009, and extended by nine months in late 2010. Of the original $11.3 billion IMF SBA, $3.6 billion is yet to be disbursed; the program was placed on hold in August 2010 because Islamabad had failed to implement required revenue and power sector reforms. Any prospective second IMF program is likely to come with more stringent conditions, including restructuring of numerous public sector enterprises. Moreover, in May 2011, security concerns spurred the IMF to put off negotiations with Pakistani officials, further delaying disbursement of remaining support funds.[183] Pakistan reportedly has sought U.S. help to "influence" the IMF to relax its conditions and release the outstanding tranches. One article claimed Pakistani officials had "begged" Secretary Clinton for such consideration during her October 2011 visit to Islamabad, but it is considered unlikely that the United States will intervene.[184]

Repayment of IMF loans will place huge constraints on Islamabad's federal budget, which is burdened by perpetually low revenue generation.[185] For most observers, this is caused by what essentially is mass tax evasion by the country's economic elite, and is exacerbated by a federal budget overemphasizing military spending. Secretary Clinton is among the U.S. officials critical of Pakistan's 9% tax-to-GDP ratio, one of the lowest in the world.[186] The government sought to implement a Reformed General Sales Tax initiative in 2011, but to date has been unable to win sufficient parliamentary support for what are considered modest changes. Likewise, the government's early 2011 effort to lower fuel subsidies spurred virulent reaction and led to political turmoil when an important PPP coalition partner withdrew its support.

Meanwhile, electricity shortages are behind much of Pakistan's economic deterioration: medium- and small-scale textile businesses, unable to operate their own generators, increasingly are being forced too shut down due to lack of power. Shortfalls in electricity supply have led to unannounced outages of up to 20 hours per day in parts of the country. Public protests over gas shortages have turned violent at times: in May 2012, thousands of angry citizens took to the streets of Lahore and other Punjabi cities, ransacking the offices of politicians and the main power agency, and torching vehicles.[187] Yet public opinion surveys show Pakistanis worrying

---

[183] By some accounts, IMF officials are privately angry with Pakistani officials for making allegedly false claims about tax reforms (see, for example, "IMF Considers Pakistan Economic Teams Deceitful, Liars," *Daily Times* (Lahore), April 26, 2011).

[184] "Looking For IMF Help, Pakistan Approaches US," *Express Tribune* (Karachi), November 1, 2011.

[185] Nearly half of Pakistan's approximately $27 billion FY2011/2012 federal budget—released in June 2011—was marked for loan repayments. The budget cut subsidies by more than half, raising prices for energy and other essential items. Planned defense spending was boosted by 12% over the previous fiscal year with a budget of nearly $4.9 billion in 2011.

[186] Secretary Clinton has called the issue "a real pet peeve" of hers, telling a House panel, "[I]t is very hard to accept helping a country that won't help itself by taxing its richest citizens" ("House Appropriations Subcommittee on State, Foreign Operations, and Related Programs Holds Hearing on the Proposed Fiscal 2012 Appropriations for the State Department," CQ Transcriptions, March 10, 2011).

[187] Chronic and severe electricity shortages are blamed on low government pricing, outdated transmission systems, and bureaucratic obstacles to completing new generation projects. Underinvestment in power stations and a deterioration of the distribution network during the 1999-2008 Musharraf era are also seen as having instigated the crisis ("Pakistan's Economy Starts to Unravel," *Financial Times* (London), October 13, 2011; "Power Protesters Go On Rampage," *Daily Times* (Lahore), May 11, 2102).

---

most about inflation; one poll found a majority of 52% calling inflation the single most important problem facing the country, well ahead of both unemployment and terrorism.[188]

Current Status and IFI Assessments

Pakistan's economy grew by 2.4% in the fiscal year ending June 2011 despite the devastating floods that opened FY2011. According to IHS Global Insight, "Onerous public debt, persistent double-digit inflation, and severe energy shortages will continue crippling growth in the near term." The State Bank of Pakistan conceded that the flooding "cannot mask the structural deficiencies in Pakistan's economy," especially chronically low tax revenues and acute power shortages. Long-standing plans to implement a reformed general sales tax, broaden the income tax net to include agriculture and services, and phase out government subsidy programs remain delayed, and power outages are estimated to reduce GDP growth by up to 4%, given concentrated impact on manufacturing. The Bank is locate a clear central cause of these "In the final analysis, all the economic problems highlighted above can be traced to poor governance."[189]

International financial institutions (IFIs) regularly issue assessments of the Pakistani economy. A November 2011 World Bank "Country Partnership Strategy Report" for FY2010-FY2014 acknowledged that the Islamabad government has faced many daunting challenges and also noted that international donors face new challenges following the 18th Amendment's devolution of key functions to provincial governments. It finds a deteriorated fiscal situation and an absence of hoped for governance improvements. By this assessment, the outlook is negative as overall macroeconomic risks continue to be significant. The World Bank recommends a focus on accelerating progress in human development sectors such as education and health, and warns that poverty alleviation gains of the early and mid-2000s are at risk in lieu of renewed growth.[190]

A February 2012 IMF report bluntly stated that,

> On current policies, Pakistan's near- and middle-term prospects are not good. Growth would remain too low to absorb the large number of new entrants into the labor force, inflation would remain high, and the external position would weaken significantly. ... The current mix of large fiscal deficits and accommodative monetary policy is increasingly unsustainable.

The IMF recommends urgent policy action to 1) strengthen public finances through revenue mobilization; 2) reform the energy sector to reduce power shortages; and 3) undertake financial measures that would reduce inflation and safeguard financial sector stability.[191]

A key aspiration for Pakistani leaders is to acquire better access to Western markets. With the security situation deterring foreign investors, exports, especially from the key textile sector, may be key to any future Pakistani recovery. Islamabad has continued to press Washington and European capitals for reduced tariffs on textile exports, especially following massive flood damage to Pakistan's cotton crop. By some accounts, the textile sector directly employs 3.5 million Pakistanis and accounts for 40% of urban factory jobs. Pakistani officials and business

---

[188] See the February 27, 2012, results at http://www.gallup.com.pk/pollsshow.php?id=2012-02-27.

[189] See the "Economic Outlook" chapter of the December 19, 2011, report at http://www.sbp.org.pk/reports/annual/arFY11/Economic_Outlook.pdf.

[190] See http://siteresources.worldbank.org/PAKISTANEXTN/Resources/293051-1298387688762/CPSPRNov21.pdf.

[191] Ibid.

leaders estimate that abolishing American tariffs, which currently average 17% on cotton apparel, would boost their country's exports by $5 billion annually.[192]

Domestic Political Setting and Instability

Overview

Democracy has fared poorly in Pakistan, and is marked by tripartite power struggles among presidents, prime ministers, and army chiefs. The country has endured direct military rule for more than half of its 65 years of existence. A bicameral Parliament is the locus of federal power under the constitution, with a 342-seat National Assembly and a 100-seat Senate. Members are elected to five-year terms by direct election; a President is indirectly elected and also serves a five-year term. President Zardari was elected in September 2008. See **Table 4** for current National Assembly composition.

More than four years after Pakistan's relatively credible March 2008 national elections seated a civilian government led by the Pakistan People's Party (PPP) of assassinated former Prime Minister Benazir Bhutto, the country's military establishment still wields decisive influence over Pakistan's foreign policy and national security policies. Meanwhile, the PPP-led coalition has struggled merely to stay in power and has been unable to rein in the security agencies or enact other major social or economic reforms. Moreover, a judiciary empowered by the 2008 "Lawyer's Movement" in support of Chief Justice Iftikhar Chaudhry has continued to do battle with the executive branch and seeks to pursue corruption charges against an array of politicians, including President Zardari himself, a deeply unpopular figure among Pakistanis. Independent analysts have warned that, if it is not halted, Pakistan's perpetual political turmoil could lead to economic chaos, given especially the widening budget and balance of payments deficits.[193]

In 2010 and 2011, serious threats to the PPP's majority status and to the very existence of its government arose due to fractious coalition politics. The Jamaat Ulema Islami (JUI)—a small but influential Islamist party—and the Karachi-based Muttahida Quami Movement (MQM) both have withdrawn and then rejoined the coalition in reaction to rising fuel prices, inflation, and perceived government mismanagement. Three times in 2011 the MQM withdrew, then rejoined the ruling coalition. Loss of the MQM's 25 seats removes that coalition's parliamentary majority, which could have led to government collapse. Most observers concluded that each withdrawal was an effort to extract maximum concessions in the form of greater administrative control for the MQM in its Karachi base.

---

[192] "Pakistan Seeks Help for Its Textiles," *Wall Street Journal*, August 19, 2010.

[193] See, for example, Maleeha Lodhi, "Looming Economic Storm?" (op-ed), *News* (Karachi), January 24, 2012.

Figure 5. Current Representation in Pakistan's National Assembly by Party

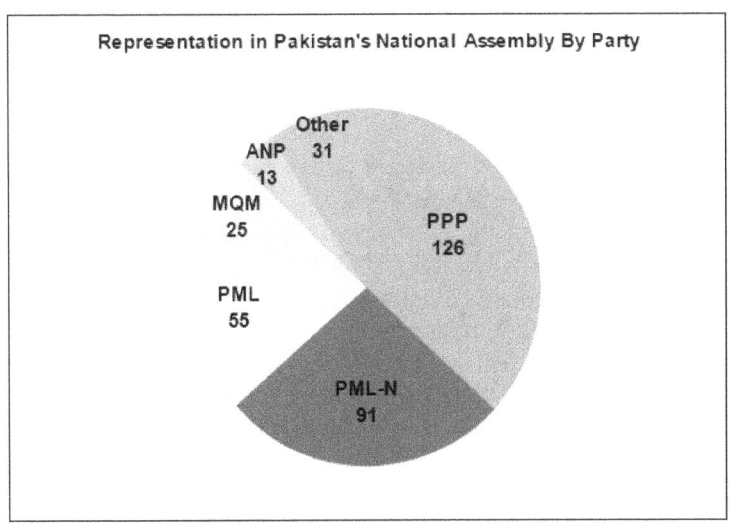

Representation in Pakistan's National Assembly By Party

Source: Election Commission of Pakistan.

In May 2011, the PPP's standing was strengthened through a new alliance with the Pakistan Muslim League-Q (PML-Q) faction, former parliamentary supporters of Pervez Musharraf. This faction recently merged with a smaller PML group and reverted to the original PML name. the party's considerable support in the Punjab province and its agreement to contest the next general elections as PPP allies bolstered the ruling party's status and could represent a threat to that of Nawaz Sharif's PML faction, the PML-Nawaz, or PNL-N. The secular Pashtun nationalist Awami National Party (ANP) is a PPP coalition ally that also runs the government of the Khyber Pakhtunkhwa province.

Senate elections in February 2012 were crucial to Zardari's political safety, as PPP gains ensured that party's control of the Senate through 2015. The ruling party increased its significant plurality and is now in a position to block legislation even if it loses in National Assembly polls expected in late 2012 or early 2013.[194]

The circumstances of OBL's death were hugely embarrassing for the Pakistani military and led to rare domestic criticism of that institution, traditionally the country's most respected. This in turn created an opening in which Pakistan's civilian leaders might wrest more control over the country's foreign and national security policies. With the embarrassment of the May 2011 Mehran naval base attack compounded by scandals involving apparent abuse of power and human rights, media criticism of the security establishment continued at unprecedented levels throughout the year. Yet, to date, there has been little sign that the civilians would take advantage of these openings; rather, they have rallied behind the security services and made no calls for the resignations of either the Army or ISI Chiefs. Parliament did seat a commission to investigate how bin Laden had found refuge in Pakistan and how American forces were able to penetrate Pakistani territory, but the body's initial lack of focus and cohesion diminished expectations that its work could lead to greater civilian authority. As discussed in the "'Memogate'" section above, civil-military tensions aggravated by the May 2011 bin Laden raid appear to have brought the country close to yet another military coup in late 2011.

---

[194] "Pakistan Governing Party Makes Big Gains in Senate," *New York Times*, March 2, 2012.

Recent Political Developments

Prime Minister's Conviction for Contempt of Court

Still more political upheaval came in early 2012 with Prime Minister Gilani facing contempt charges for his failure to abide by Supreme Court orders that he request that Swiss authorities reopen a longstanding corruption case against President Zardari. Gilani had contended that, as president, Zardari was immune from any prosecution, an argument the court refused to accept. In January the court, led by Chief Justice Iftikhar Chaudhry, issued a contempt notice against the Prime Minister. In April, justices found Gilani guilty of contempt, but made an apparent tactical retreat by sentencing him to only the time it took for the court to adjourn (less than one minute). Gilani has since refused opposition demands that he resign, but many legal scholars predict that he will be disqualified from holding office at some point after the appeal period expires in June, although the Speaker of the National Assembly has determined the Prime Minister is not subject to disqualification.[195] A State Department spokesman had no comment beyond calling the case a domestic political issue for Pakistan.

The Rise of Imran Khan

Late 2011 saw the surprising rise of a new political star in Pakistan, former cricket hero Imran Khan and his Pakistan Tehreek-e-Insaf (PTI or Pakistan Movement for Justice) party. Although he has been a national-level political figure since 1996, his PTI was considered a "party of one" with minimal representation in Parliament (his seat only). Yet in late 2011 he was able to attract support from young and middle-class Pakistanis by riding a wave of anti-corruption and anti-American sentiment. Khan's rallies in Lahore in October and Karachi in December each attracted huge and enthusiastic crowds of more than 100,000. The PTI has since won notable converts from both of Pakistan's major national parties. With especially strong support in Punjab, Khan represents a particular threat to the votebank of former Prime Minister Nawaz Sharif's Pakistan Muslim League offshoot (the PML-N).

While it is considered unlikely that Khan could win enough seats in parliamentary elections expected in early 2013 to become Prime Minister, he may well become a "kingmaker" in future governance arrangements. Khan has vowed that if he comes to power he would cut off U.S. aid flows and end conflict with the Pakistani Taliban "in 90 days—guaranteed." He has also promised to "end big corruption in 90 days."[196] Such pronouncements seem outlandish to many observers, and Khan has expressed sympathy for Islamist causes and is rumored to have at least tacit backing from the military. Yet there is widespread agreement that Khan's meteoric rise in late 2011 reflected the Pakistani public's hunger for honest politicians not beholden to the country's entrenched, dynastic mainstream parties.[197]

---

[195] "PM's Disqualification: What the Legal Experts Think," *Express Tribune* (Karachi), May 9, 2012; "Gilani Cannot Be Disqualified Under Article 63: Speaker NA," *Express Tribune* (Karachi), May 24, 2012.

[196] "Imran Khan Predicts 'A Revolution' in Pakistani Politics," *Guardian* (London), November 6, 2011; "Massive Khan Rally Defies Pakistan Ruling Party," Reuters, December 25, 2011.

[197] Shahid Javed Burki, "Imran Khan's Political Rise," Institute for South Asian Studies Insights No. 148, December 27, 2011; Moshin Hamid, "A Kennedy for Pakistan?," *New York Review of Books*, March 22, 2012.

An Islamist Rightwing Resurgence

A final domestic political development of particular concern to international observers has been the reemergence of Pakistan's conservative Islamist political forces under the rubric of the newly-formed Difa-e-Pakistan (DPC or Defend Pakistan Council). Comprised of more than 40 Islamist and rightwing parties—among them several extremist groups supposedly banned by the Pakistani government—the DPC has held large-scale street rallies and is at the cutting edge of demands that Islamabad end its cooperation with the United States, as well as halt any rapprochement with India.[198] Hafiz Saeed, leader of the Lashkar-e-Taiba (LeT) terrorist group behind the November 2008 Mumbai attack in India, is among those appearing openly at DPC rallies.[199] The DPC strenuously opposes reopening of the GLOCs, considering such a move "akin to helping the allied forces prolong their stay in Afghanistan," and contends that both the United States and India are "involved in Baluchistan's insurgency."[200] Meanwhile, other officially banned terrorist groups appear to thrive with impunity.[201] Anti-American rhetoric has become valuable political currency for any Pakistani politician seeking patriotic credentials, and some analysts see Pakistan's security services benefitting from and possibly supporting the DPC's rise as a tool of leverage against both the United States and Pakistan's own civilian leaders.[202]

Human Rights Issues

Pakistan is the setting for serious reported human rights abuses, some of them perpetrated and/or sanctioned by the state itself. According to the U.S. Department of State, although Pakistan's civilian government has taken some positive steps, the overall human rights situation there remains poor, and that lack of government accountability remains a pervasive problem; abuses often go unpunished, fostering a culture of impunity.[203] According to the May 2012 *Country Reports on Human Rights for 2011*,

> The most serious human rights problems were extrajudicial killings, torture, and disappearances committed by security forces, as well as by militant, terrorist, and extremist groups .... Other human rights problems included poor prison conditions, instances of arbitrary detention, lengthy pretrial detention, a weak criminal justice system, insufficient training for prosecutors and criminal investigators, a lack of judicial independence in the lower courts, and infringements on citizens' privacy rights. Harassment of journalists, some censorship, and self-censorship continued. There were some restrictions on freedom of assembly and some limits on freedom of movement. The number of religious freedom violations and discrimination against religious minorities increased, including some violations sanctioned by law. Corruption was widespread within the government and the

---

[198] "In Pakistan, Rightwing Alliance is Revived," Associated Press, February 15, 2012; "New Pakistan Extremist Movement Leaves Government Powerless as it Chants 'Death to America,'" *Telegraph* (London), February 26, 2012.

[199] The U.S. government has expressed concerned about Saeed's public appearances (see http://www.state.gov/r/pa/prs/ps/2012/02/184060 htm).

[200] DPC press release, April 16, 2012, at http://www.difaepakistan.com.

[201] The sectarian terrorist Sipah-e-Sahaba—now known as Ahle Sunnat wal Jamaat—held an October 2011 rally in the heart of the Pakistani capital, where up to 10,000 activists expressed support for the army and opposition to further cooperation with the United States ("Banned Islamists Rally in Full View in Pakistan's Capital," McClatchy News, October 7, 2011).

[202] Arif Rafiq, "The Emergence of the Difa-E-Pakistan Islamist Coalition," *CTC Sentinel*, March 22, 2012.

[203] *Country Reports on Human Rights Practices for 2011*, released May 2012.

---

police forces, and the government made few attempts to combat the problem. Rape, domestic violence, sexual harassment, "honor" crimes, abuse, and discrimination against women remained serious problems. Child abuse and commercial sexual exploitation of children persisted. Widespread human trafficking—including forced and bonded labor—was a serious problem. Societal discrimination against national, ethnic, and racial minorities continued, as did discrimination based on caste, sexual orientation, gender identity, and HIV status. Lack of respect for worker rights continued. ... Violence, abuse, and social and religious intolerance by militant organizations, and other nongovernmental actors contributed to a culture of lawlessness in some parts of the country.[204]

Among this litany of serious and ongoing human rights abuses, watchdog groups commonly rank Pakistan as the world's most dangerous country for journalists, even as a raucous free press has emerged in the past decade. "Disappearances" and extrajudicial killings by Pakistani security forces elicited acute U.S. concerns in late 2010 when evidence of abuses came to light. The Obama Administration has declared that it will abide by "Leahy amendment" provisions by withholding train and equip funding for several Pakistani army units believed to be complicit in human rights abuses.[205]

Laws prohibiting blasphemy in Pakistan are meant to protect Islamic holy persons, beliefs, customs, and objects from insult or defilement. They are widely popular with the public. Yet they are criticized by human rights groups as discriminatory and arbitrary in their use, which often arises in the context of personal vendettas, and can involve little or no persuasive evidence. The laws again came under scrutiny in late 2010 when a Pakistani Christian woman was sentenced to death for what seemed to many a minor offense. International human rights groups issued newly urgent calls for the law's repeal, and President Zardari himself vowed to personally review the case. Yet the PPP-led government backed away from reform proposals after Islamist hardline groups, including some with links to terrorist organizations, were able to rally a host of protestors. As noted above, two of the most vocal government proponents of reforming the laws were assassinated earlier in 2011. The only other high-profile national politician pursuing reform efforts, National Assembly member Sherry Rehman, was forced to withdraw her legislative proposal after her PPP leaders announced that no reforms would be undertaken.

U.S. Foreign Assistance and Coalition Support Reimbursements[206]

In 2001, Congress renewed large U.S. assistance packages to Pakistan. By the end of 2011, Congress had appropriated about $15.3 billion in overt assistance over ten years, including more than $8.3 billion in development and humanitarian aid, and nearly $7 billion for security-related programs (see **Table 1**). In 2009, both chambers of Congress passed their own Pakistan-specific bills authorizing increased nonmilitary aid to Pakistan (to $1.5 billion per year for five years) and

---

[204] Ibid., at http://www.state.gov/j/drl/rls/hrrpt/humanrightsreport/index.htm?dynamic_load_id=186473.

[205] Sec. 620J of the Foreign Assistance Act of 1961 (P.L. 87-195, as amended), also known as the Leahy Amendment, states that "No assistance shall be furnished under this Act or the Arms Export Control Act to any unit of the security forces of a foreign country if the Secretary of State has credible evidence that such unit has committed gross violations of human rights."

[206] For broader discussion, see CRS Report R41856, *Pakistan: U.S. Foreign Assistance*, by Susan B. Epstein and K. Alan Kronstadt.

placing certain conditions on future security-related aid to that country. The Enhanced Partnership with Pakistan Act (EPPA) of 2009, also known as the "Kerry-Lugar-Berman" (KLB) bill for its main sponsors, became P.L. 111-73. Earlier that year, Congress also established a new Pakistan Counterinsurgency Capability Fund (PCCF) that is meant to enhance the ability of Pakistani security forces to effectively combat militancy. Moreover, since FY2002 Congress has appropriated billions of dollars to reimburse Pakistan (and other nations) for its operational and logistical support of U.S.-led counterterrorism operations. At nearly $9 billion paid to date, these "coalition support funds" have accounted for more than one-third of all overt U.S. financial transfers to Pakistan since 2001. In recent years, more careful oversight of such disbursements reportedly has led to a major increase in the rate of rejected claims.[207]

The Administration's congressionally mandated Pakistan Assistance Strategy Report, issued in December 2009, laid out the principal objectives of nonmilitary U.S. assistance to Pakistan (to help "in building a stable, secure, and prosperous Pakistan"), a general description of the programs and projects designed to achieve these goals, and a plan for monitoring and evaluating the effort. For FY2010-FY2014, it proposed to devote $3.5 billion—nearly half of the $7.5 billion of the aid authorized by the EPPA—to "high-impact, high-visibility" infrastructure programs, especially in the energy and agriculture sectors. Most recently, Washington is considering making grants to help the Pakistani government launch construction of the planned Diamer Basha dam in the country's far northeast. The Asian Development Bank is taking the lead on the roughly $12 billion project which, when completed in eight or more years, could generate 4,500 megawatts of electricity, enough to fill the country's entire current shortfall.[208]

The Administration reports having disbursed about $855 million in civilian aid funds during FY2011, excluding emergency humanitarian assistance. Roughly half of such aid is distributed directly through Pakistani government institutions. Still, the majority of appropriated KLB funds have not been spent, in large part because of concerns about corruption and the capacity of Pakistan's government and contractors to effectively oversee aid projects, and confusion over priorities. The delay serves to reinforce Pakistani perceptions that the United States cannot be relied upon to follow through on its promises.

Security-related U.S. assistance to Pakistan has included provision of extensive "train and equip" programs, but these were largely suspended in mid-2011. Major U.S. arms transfers to Pakistan since 2001 have included items useful for counterterrorism operations, along with a number of "big ticket" platforms more suited to conventional warfare. Under multiple authorities, Pakistan has received helicopters, infantry arms, and a wide array of other equipment. Pakistani officials have complained that U.S.-supplied defense equipment, especially that most needed for counterinsurgency operations such as attack and utility helicopters, was too slow in coming. Security assistance to Pakistan's civilian sector is aimed at strengthening the country's law enforcement capabilities through basic police training, provision of advanced identification systems, and establishment of a new Counterterrorism Special Investigation Group.

As noted above, the circumstances of OBL's death and subsequent developments have had major impact on both Administration and congressional perceptions of the utility of current U.S. aid

---

[207] Pakistan reportedly has "routinely" submitted "unsubstantiated" or "exaggerated" claims, and denial rates climbed from less than 2% in 2005 to 44% in 2009 ("U.S. Balks at Pakistani Bills," *Wall Street Journal*, May 17, 2011).

[208] "US to Cut Pakistan Aid Projects," *Financial Times* (London), June 2, 2011; "Pakistan Inaugurates Huge Dam Project, Hoping U.S. Will Help With Funds," McClatchy News, October 18, 2011.

programs. A substantive reevaluation of aid levels—and of the bilateral relationship more generally—began in 2011. Such rethinking has become evident in significant reductions, as well as new restrictions and conditions, in pending FY2013 legislation (see the **Appendix**), and congressional figures have issued some of the strongest criticisms of Pakistan as a U.S. ally seen in decades. There appears to be growing recognition among observers that U.S. military aid has done little to stem Islamist militancy in Pakistan and may even hinder that country's economic and political development. Many of these analysts thus urge U.S. policy targeting effective nonmilitary aid, perhaps especially that which would strengthen Pakistan's civil society.[209]

Table I. Direct Overt U.S. Aid Appropriations and Military Reimbursements to Pakistan, FY2002-FY2013

(rounded to the nearest millions of dollars)

Program or Account	FY2002-FY2006	FY2007	FY2008	FY2009	FY2010	FY2011	FY2012 (est.)	Program or Account Total	FY2013 (req.)
1206	28	14	131d	139d	—	—	—	312	—
CN	32	49	54	47	43	39	h	264	h
CSFa	4,947	731	1,019	685	1,499	f	f	8,881f	f
FMF	971	297	298	300	294	295	295	2,750	350
IMET	7	2	2	2	5	4	5	27	6
INCLE	224	24	22	88	170	114	116	758	124
NADR	33	10	10	13	24	25	21	136	19
PCF/PCCF	—	—	—	400	700e	800g	800	2,700g	800
Total Security-Related	**6,242**	**1,127**	**1,536**	**1,674**	**2,735**	**1,277**	**1,237**	**15,828**	**1,299**
CSH/GHCS	105	22	30	34	30	28	—	249	—
DA	161	95	30	—	—	—	—	286	—
ESF	1,639c	394	347	1,114	1,292	919	865	6,570	928
Food Aidb	133	—	50	55	124	51	9	422	—
HRDF	6	11	—	—	—	—	—	17	—
IDA	70	50	50	103	232	145	—	650	—
MRA	38	4	—	61	49	—	—	152	—
Total Economic-Related	**2,152**	**576**	**507**	**1,367**	**1,727**	**1,143**	**874**	**8,346**	**928**
Grand Total	**8,394**	**1,703**	**2,043**	**3,041**	**4,462**	**2,420**	**2,111**	**24,174**	**2,227**

Sources: U.S. Departments of State, Defense, and Agriculture; U.S. Agency for International Development. Final obligation and disbursement totals are typically lower than program account totals.

Abbreviations:

[209] See, for example, Colin Cookman, et al., "The Limits of U.S. Assistance to Pakistan," Center for American Progress, July 2011; Timothy Hoyt, "Pakistan, an Ally By Any Other Name," *Proceedings*, July 2011.

1206: Section 1206 of the National Defense Authorization Act (NDAA) for FY2006 (P.L. 109-163, global train and equip)

CN: Counternarcotics Funds (Pentagon budget)

CSF: Coalition Support Funds (Pentagon budget)

CSH: Child Survival and Health (Global Health and Child Survival, or GHCS, from FY2010)

DA: Development Assistance

ESF: Economic Support Funds

FMF: Foreign Military Financing

HRDF: Human Rights and Democracy Funds

IDA: International Disaster Assistance (Pakistani earthquake, flood, and internally displaced persons relief)

IMET: International Military Education and Training

INCLE: International Narcotics Control and Law Enforcement (includes border security)

MRA: Migration and Refugee Assistance (also includes Emergency Migration and Refugee Assistance or ERMA)

NADR: Nonproliferation, Anti-Terrorism, Demining, and Related (the majority allocated for Pakistan is for anti-terrorism assistance)

PCF/PCCF: Pakistan Counterinsurgency Fund/Counterinsurgency Capability Fund (PCF overseen by the Pentagon, PCCF overseen by State)

Notes:

a. CSF is Pentagon funding to reimburse Pakistan for its support of U.S. military operations; it is technically not foreign assistance.

b. P.L.480 Title I (loans), P.L.480 Title II (grants), and Section 416(b) of the Agricultural Act of 1949, as amended (surplus agricultural commodity donations). Food aid totals do not include freight costs.

c. Congress authorized Pakistan to use the FY2003 and FY2004 ESF allocations to cancel a total of $1.5 billion in debt to the U.S. government.

d. Includes $75 million for FY2008 and $25 million for FY2009 to train and equip Pakistan's Frontier Corps as authorized by Section 1206 of the NDAA for FY2008 (P.L. 110-181).

e. These funds were appropriated in and became available on the final day of FY2009.

f. Congress appropriated $1.6 billion for FY2011 and $1.69 billion for FY2012, and the Administration has requested $1.75 billion for FY2013, in additional CSF for all U.S. coalition partners. Pakistan has in the past received more than three-quarters of such funds. Disbursements to Pakistan have been on hold since December 2010, with approximately $600 million approved for the first two quarters of FY2011.

g. In July 2011, the Administration suspended approximately $440 million in planned PCF payments following the Pakistani government's expulsion of most American military trainers. This amount has not been deducted from the FY2011 total.

h. This funding is "requirements-based"; there are no pre-allocation data.

Appendix. Notable Related Provisions in FY2013 Legislation[210]

Three major bills authorizing and appropriating U.S. spending in FY2013 contain important Pakistan-related provisions, including new reporting and certification requirements based on more stringent conditions.

First, the National Defense Authorization Act for FY2013 (**H.R. 4310**, passed by the full House on May 18, 2012), would

- prohibit the Secretary of Defense from preferential procurement of goods or services from Pakistan until such time as that country's government reopens the ground lines of communication (GLOCs) to Afghanistan (Sec. 821(d));

- limit FY2013 CSF payments to Pakistan to no more than $650 million (Sec. 1211(b));

- withhold CSF payments to Pakistan unless the Secretary of Defense reports to Congress on the claims process, any new conditions Pakistan has placed on use of its GLOCs, and estimates any differences in transit costs from FY2011 to FY2013 (Sec. 1211(c));

- withhold FY2012 CSF payments to Pakistan unless the Secretary certifies that the Islamabad government is 1) supporting counterterrorism operations against Al Qaeda, its associated movements, the Haqqani Network, and other domestic and foreign terrorist organizations; 2) dismantling IED networks; 3) preventing nuclear-related proliferation; and 4) issuing visas in a timely manner for official U.S. visitors (Sec. 1211(c); and

- limit the obligation or disbursement of FY2013 PCF funds to 10% of those appropriated or transferred unless the Secretary of Defense, with the concurrence of the Secretary of State, reports to Congress an updated strategy on utilization of the Fund, metrics for determining relevant progress, and a strategy for enhancing Pakistan's efforts to counter IEDs (Sec. 1217).

Second, as approved by the Senate Appropriations Committee on May 24, 2012, **S. 3241**, a bill to fund the State Department and foreign operations for FY2013, contains provisions that would

- provide $50 million for the PCCF (about 6% of both the amount requested by the Administration and the amount appropriated for FY2012), but only if the Secretary of State certifies that Pakistan has reopened the GLOCs to Afghanistan and that the funds can be used efficiently and effectively;

- withhold all funds appropriated for Pakistan under ESF, INCLE, FMF, and PCCF unless the Secretary of State certifies that Pakistan is (1) cooperating with the United States in counterterrorism efforts against the Haqqani Network, the Quetta Shura Taliban, Lashkar-e-Taiba, Jaish-e-Mohammed, Al Qaeda, and other

---

[210] See also CRS Report R42116, *Pakistan: U.S. Foreign Aid Conditions, Restrictions, and Reporting Requirements*, by Susan B. Epstein and K. Alan Kronstadt.

domestic and foreign terrorist organizations; (2) not supporting terrorist activities against United States or coalition forces in Afghanistan, and Pakistan's military and intelligence agencies are not intervening extra-judicially into political and judicial processes in Pakistan; (3) dismantling IED networks; (4) preventing nuclear-related proliferation; (5) implementing policies to protect judicial independence and rule of law; (6) issuing visas in a timely manner for official U.S. visitors; and (7) providing humanitarian organizations access to detainees, internally displaced persons, and other Pakistani civilians affected by the conflict (Sec. 7046(c)(1)) (the Secretary may waive these requirements if doing so is important to U.S. national security interests);

- limit total State Department aid to Pakistan to about $800 million (roughly 36% of the Administration's request), including no more than $375 million for ESF, $100 million for INCLE, and $250 million for FMF (Sec. 7046(c)(2));

- further withhold $33 million of appropriated FMF funds unless the Secretary of State certifies that Dr. Shakil Afridi has been released from prison and cleared of all charged relating to the assistance provided to the United States in locating Osama bin Laden (Sec. 7046(c)(2)(G)); and

- require the Secretary of State to submit to Congress a spend plan for assistance to Pakistan to include achievable and sustainable goals, benchmarks for measuring progress, and expected results regarding furthering development in Pakistan, countering extremism, and establishing conditions conducive to the rule of law and transparent and accountable governance; report biannually on the status of achieving that plan's goals and benchmarks; and recommend that the Secretary suspend all assistance to Pakistan if this report finds Pakistan is failing to make measureable progress toward stated goals and benchmarks (Sec. 7046(c)(3)).

The bill provides that $100 million of the ESF funds may be used by the President for Overseas Contingency Operations if so designated by Congress.

Third, as approved by the House Appropriations Committee on May 25, 2012, **H.R. 5857**, a bill to fund the State Department and foreign operations for FY2013, contains provisions that would

- provide no funding for PCCF;

- withhold all funds appropriated for Pakistan under ESF, INCLE, FMF, and PCCF unless the Secretary of State certifies that Pakistan is 1) cooperating with the United States in counterterrorism efforts against the Haqqani Network, the Quetta Shura Taliban, Lashkar-e-Taiba, Jaish-e-Mohammed, Al Qaeda, and other domestic and foreign terrorist organizations; 2) not supporting terrorist activities against United States or coalition forces in Afghanistan, and Pakistan's military and intelligence agencies are not intervening extra-judicially into political and judicial processes in Pakistan; 3) dismantling IED networks; 4) preventing nuclear-related proliferation; 5) issuing visa in a timely manner for official U.S. visitors; and 6) providing humanitarian organizations access to detainees, internally displaced persons, and other Pakistani civilians affected by the conflict (Sec. 7046(c)(1)) (unlike S. 3241, this provision does not include a national security waiver);

- require the Secretary of State to submit to Congress a spend plan for assistance to Pakistan to include achievable and sustainable goals, benchmarks for measuring progress, and expected results regarding furthering development in Pakistan, countering extremism, and establishing conditions conducive to the rule of law and transparent and accountable governance; report biannually on the status of achieving that plan's goals and benchmarks; and recommend that the Secretary suspend all assistance to Pakistan if this report finds Pakistan is failing to make measureable progress toward stated goals and benchmarks (Sec. 7046(b)(3));

- allow ESF funds, notwithstanding any other provision of law, for cross border stabilization and development programs between Afghanistan and Pakistan or between either country and the central Asian republics (Sec. 7046(c)).

- allow INCLE and FMF funds to be transferred to PCCF and remain available until September 30, 2014 as long as the Secretary of State notifies Congress 15 days before such action and specifies source of funds and implementation plan. Obligation of such funds are subject to Sec. 7046(b) of this act.

Author Contact Information

K. Alan Kronstadt
Specialist in South Asian Affairs
akronstadt@crs.loc.gov, 7-5415